JOSEPH PRIESTLEY

A COURSE OF LECTURES ON THE THEORY OF LANGUAGE AND UNIVERSAL GRAMMAR

1762

A Scolar Press Facsimile

THE SCOLAR PRESS LIMITED
MENSTON, ENGLAND
1970

THE SCOLAR PRESS LIMITED
20 Main Street, Menston, Yorkshire, England

Printed in Great Britain by
The Scolar Press Limited
Menston, Yorkshire, England

NOTE

Joseph Priestley's lectures on the theory of language were delivered at the Warrington Academy where he had been appointed tutor in languages and belles-lettres. To this period also belong the lectures on history (*An essay on a Course of Liberal Education*, 1765; *Lectures on History*, 1788), and his influential *Rudiments of English Grammar* (1761). The important point about Priestley's approach to language was his confident assumption that it is "founded upon Science", and he is the first English writer to proclaim the study of language as a science. The importance which Priestley attached to the study of language is characteristically put in the Introduction to the work here reproduced:

> Besides, what can have a juster claim to our attention as a matter of *curiosity*, than an enquiry into the foundation of that art which is the means of preserving and bringing to perfection all other arts; an enquiry into the extent and application of a faculty which is, to a great degree, the measure of our intellectual powers; which, therefore, constitutes what is the most obvious, and at the same time a real distinction between the rational and merely animal nature; which, according to the different degrees of perfection in which it is possessed, distinguishes nations that are improved from those that

are barbarous; and which, in the same country, renders one man superior to another.

(pp. 8-9)

Priestley's lectures on language have never been reprinted separately (they were included in J. T. Rutt's collected edition of his works). The British Museum copy of the 1762 edition has numerous notes in manuscript by Andrew Kippis (1725-1795) a noncomformist friend of Priestley's. One of the copies in the Birmingham Public Library also has numerous notes in manuscript.

Reference: R. E. Crook, *A Bibliography of Joseph Priestley*, Library Association, 1966, p. 108.

A

COURSE of LECTURES

ON THE

THEORY of LANGUAGE,

AND

UNIVERSAL GRAMMAR.

By JOSEPH PRIESTLEY.

WARRINGTON:

Printed by W. EYRES,

MDCCLXII.

A D V E R T I S E M E N T.

LEST the following performance fhould, by any accident, fall into other hands than thofe for whofe ufe it is peculiarly calculated; it is neceffary to advertife in this place, that it is only intended to furnifh the lecturer with a convenient method for difcuffing the feveral fubjects of it in a more diffufe and familiar manner, and by no means to be a full and compleat fet of lectures, that need no further enlargement.

INTRODUCTION.

L A N G U A G E, whether fpoken or written, is properly termed an *Art ;* the rules of it being calculated to direct our practice: and it is, without all difpute, an art of unfpeakable importance to mankind; as beings who, from the commencement to the clofe of this mortal life, can hardly fub- fift but as members of fome particular com- munity, and are, moreover, capable of the moft extenfive focial connections.

GRAMMARS are books that contain the rules and precepts of this art: and, not- withftanding the art of fpeech is always

learned

learned at firft, and that of fpeaking any particular language may be learned at any time of life, as all other arts may be learned, by *imitation* only, without precept; the rules of Grammar, when perfons are capable of ufing them, do very much facilitate the acquiring this art, and are of great ufe in order to make a perfon more exactly and extenfively acquainted with a language that was learned at firft without their affiftance. Thus the Grammars of the *Hebrew*, *Greek*, *Latin*, *Englifh* and other tongues contain all the rules and precepts neceffary to make a perfon underftand the ftructure of thofe languages; in order to enable him, either to ufe them with accuracy himfelf, or underftand another perfon who ufes them.

All *Art* is founded on *Science*, or the knowledge of the materials employed in them and their fitnefs for the ufes to which they

are

are applied. And though many arts were found out by accident, without any previous knowledge of thofe parts of nature on which they depend, it is ufeful to trace arts to their natural principles, and to be able to comprehend the reafon of the beneficial effects they have in practice: for this knowledge leads to the means of perfecting and extending the arts.

Thus *Medicine* is the art of curing difeafes, and though the methods of cure, in moft particular cafes, might be found out by chance, and many tollerably fuccefsful practitioners never trouble themfelves about the theory of Phyfic, yet cures certainly depend upon the nature of the human body and of the medicines applied to it: fince their mutual action, with the beneficial confequences of it, muft have been agreeable to the ufual courfe of nature: and it is wor-

A 3 thy

thy the attention of the profeffors of that art to confider it as a fcience, to trace out the natural caufes of the diforders of the human body, to underftand the properties of the feveral articles of the *materia medica* they make ufe of, and confider their mutual influences; fince, knowing the fubject they act upon, and thofe they act with, they may be better able to predict and procure any defired event.

In like manner is the *art of language* founded upon fcience; and it is a matter both of curiofity and ufefulnefs to enquire into the natural powers of thofe founds and characters which are the inftruments of it, to confider the modifications they are capable of, and their fitnefs to anfwer the purpofes of a language proper for the mutual communication of fuch beings as we are.

This

This *theory* or *rationale* of language is the subject of the following course of lectures. In them it is proposed to point out the several powers and modes of expression that sounds and characters are capable of, to trace their connexion with, or relation to the ideas they represent; and to shew the actual variety of the external expressions of the same mental conceptions which different languages exhibit. This comparison will enable us to judge which is the most adaquate and convenient method of expression, will discover what is defective, and what is redundant in the structure of any particular language, and direct to the most proper method of supplying the defect, or lessening the inconveniences arising from the superfluity; and, lastly, it is only from a perfect knowledge of the theory of language in general that we can form any rational expectations of what some ingenious persons in the republick

lick of letters have conjectured may be one of the laft and greateft atchievements of human genius, viz. a *philofophical* and *univerfal language*, which fhall be the moft natural and perfect expreffion of human ideas and fentiments, and much better adapted than any language now in ufe, to anfwer all the purpofes of human life and fcience.

Befides, what can have a jufter claim to our attention as a matter of *curiofity*, than an enquiry into the foundation of that art which is the means of preferving and bringing to perfection all other arts; an enquiry into the extent and application of a faculty which is, to a great degree, the meafure of our intellectual powers; which, therefore, conftitutes what is the moft obvious, and at the fame time a real diftinction between the rational and merely animal nature; which, according

according to the different degrees of perfection in which it is poffeffed, diftinguifhes nations that are improved from thofe that are
barbarous; and which, in the fame country,
renders one man fuperior to another.

The *examples* and *illuftrations* which
there was occafion to introduce into the
following lectures, more than our own
tongue could furnifh, are defignedly brought
from thofe languages chiefly which a liberal
education among ourfelves brings us acquainted with, as *Latin, Greek, Hebrew,*
and *French:* the principles of which it is,
therefore, of more particular confequence
to the *Britifh Youth* perfectly to underftand.
This defign however hath not been fo
rigoroufly adhered to, as to exclude an account of what is curious and fingular in
the ftructure of other languages.

LECTURE

LECTURE the FIRST.

OF

ARTICULATION.

THE kind author of nature hath given to every animal that is capable of any kind of fociety, a power of communicating his fenfations and apprehenfions, at leaft, to every other animal he is connected with: and this power is more or lefs extenfive in proportion as the animal is fitted for a more perfect or imperfect ftate of fociety.

An

An animal that hath little connection with, or dependance upon any others, either of his own or a different fpecies, as he hath little to communicate, hath a power of communication proportionably fmall: but when the connections of any animal are more numerous, and the difpofitions and actions of others are of more confequence to him, it is requifite that, for his own advantage, he be furnifhed with a greater power of affecting them, by communicating his own ideas, apprehenfions, and inclinations to them.

The *inftrument* and *medium* of this communication are different, according to the different fituations of animals: in fome it being moft convenient to apply to one fenfe, and in others to another. E. G. *Fifhes*, which, it is fuppofed, have no organs of hearing, probably give all the information

information they can give to one another
by motion, perceived by the fight or feeling:
but the *air*, by means of its elafticity (whereby it is capable of tranfmitting every poffible
variety of vibration) affords to all animals
that live in it a moft convenient medium of
communication by *founds*, which are perceived by the ear.

The nature of thefe communications is
fuch as is beft fuited to the character and
occafions of each animal refpectively. The
ftrong and ravenous animals are furnifhed
with a tone of voice that infpires terrour and
confternation into thofe to whom it is di-
rected; whereas the fhrieking and wailing
note of the more timorous and defencelefs
creatures tends to infpire pity and compaffi-
on; and animals of a middle nature, that are
capable both of annoying others, and being
annoyed themfelves, have their organs formed to emit founds adapted to each condition.

The

The power of communication being, exactly proportioned to our social connections, must be nearly of the same extent with the furniture of the mind. And as the mental powers are intimately connected with the corporeal, an endeavour to exprefs an alteration in the one will produce a correspondent alteration in the other: so that from the voices and gestures of brute animals, others (and particularly those of the same species, which have the same feelings, and the same power of expreffion with themselves,) may understand the whole of what they mean to convey: and even men, who have given sufficient attention to them, may be able to decypher their meaning to a confiderable degree. Joy, forrow, furprize, with the various fubdivisions of those paffions, hope, fear, love, anger, jealoufy, and the like, as they have a strong feeling of, they have strong expreffions for: and it is probable

B   that

that their other intellectual operations are very imperfect, as they are able to give but very obscure indications of them: though dogs, horses, elephants, and some few others give very strong proofs of thinking and sagacity by their actions.

Brute animals, though capable of emitting a considerable variety of sounds, have very little power of modulating their voices; which is called ARTICULATION. Of this men are capable. It consists not only in varying the aperture of the mouth, and thereby straitening or opening the passage of the sound, or in giving a greater or less degree of force to it; but, chiefly, in checking and stopping it in a great variety of ways, by the action of the tongue, lips, palate, and teeth. The difference in the aperture of the mouth makes the different *vowels*, and the different manner in which the sound

may

may be ftopped and emitted again makes the different *confonants* of fpeech. Both vowels and confonants, when a method was found out of exprefling them in writing, were called *letters*, and a collection of all the letters belonging to any language is called the *Alphabet* of that language, from *alpha* and *beta* being the firft letters of the *Greeks*.

As the pronunciation of very few of the confonants doth intirely ftop the paffage of the found, and as the emiffion of the air in ever fo fmall a quantity, either at the mouth or noftrils, is fufficient for the propagation of fome found; moft of the confonants yield a found as well as the vowels. Thofe articulations have obtained the name of vowels, which occafion the moft manifeft aperture of the mouth, give the freeft paffage to the air, and are, confequently, attended with the moft audible found.

It

It is obfervable that dogs and other animals, not having the power of articulation,
make ufe of various *geftures*, and motions
to exprefs their meaning. With men too
geftures and poftures of the body, and particularly motions of the hands, and of the
features of the countenance, are ftrongly
affociated with particular ftates of mind; and
being in a lefs degree voluntary, are often
a furer indication of a man's real internal
feelings than words, which are more at his
command. Thefe geftures, being equally
fignificant with words, we often have recourfe to them to exprefs a paffion, or a
fimple intention, with more force.

When nature hath denied the power of
fpeech to a number of individuals we,
neverthelefs, often fee them capable of hold-
ing fomething like a converfation in
dumb-fhow, and people whofe language is
fcanty

ſcanty are obliged to help out their meaning very much by geſtures. This travellers obſerve to be the caſe with barbarous nations.

The articulations of the human voice are either *ſimple* or *complex*. The ſimple articulations are few, but the combinations of articulations in complex ſounds are almoſt infinite; ſo as not only to ſupply different terms for every thing we can expreſs, but to furniſh different nations with intirely different ſets of terms, and thereby conſtitute all the different languages which are ſpoken on the face of the earth: many of which have not only no one and the ſame word to expreſs the ſame thing, but hardly ſo much as one common ſound, though to expreſs different things.

So extenſive is the power of articulation, that ſingle letters are ſeldom made uſe of to

B 3   expreſs

exprefs any thing: they are, therefore,
generally faid to have no fignification of
themfelves. *Words,* therefore, or combinations of letters are the firft elements of
fignificant fpeech: thus in the word *hand,*
none of the letters *h, a, n,* or *d,* have any
fignification of themfelves, but the word
hand hath a determinate meaning annexed
to it.

The fame fet of founds, or alphabet of
letters, is not in ufe in all nations; becaufe mankind happened to fall early
into a different application of the organs of
fpeech, and thofe who were defcended of
any particular family or nation, or educated
among them, would learn the founds that
were in ufe in that family or nation by imitation: and as a number, much fhort of all
the modulations that the human voice is
capable of, is fufficient for all the occafions
of

of human life, there is room for very great diverſity in the articulation of different nations. *(a)*

Thoſe articulations are preferred which occaſion the leaſt difficulty to the ſpeaker, and give the leaſt pain to the hearer. Very ancient languages (as the *Hebrew*, *Arabick*, *Welch*, and even the *Greek*) do generally abound with harſh articulations; which, however, are uſually loſt when the languages ceaſe to be ſpoken; the languages that are formed out of their ruins retaining only the more eaſy and agreeable part of them. And when thoſe languages, for the purpoſes

---

(a) The *Braſilean* tongue hath not the letters *f. l. ſ.* and *z.* never joins a mute to a liquid, as *cra, pra;* and never uſes two conſonants together in the ſame word, except *mb, nd, ng.*

The *Hurons*, a North American nation, never cloſe their lips when they ſpeak; having no *labials* as *b, v, m, p* in their language.

purpoſes of literature, are at any time re-vived, it generally happens that the pro-nunciation of them is made to conform to the more convenient articulation of thoſe who learn them; and ſince the languages are no longer uſed in converſation, and con-ſequently a very accurate diſtinction of the ſound is not neceſſary to diſtinguiſh the ſenſe, the revival of harſh antiquated ſounds ſeem to be an uſeleſs and aukward practice. There is, however, this inconvenience in departing from the native pronunciation of any language, that the native harmony of it is thereby loſt.

LECTURE

LECTURE the SECOND.

Of the ORIGIN of

LETTERS.

AMAZING as is the power and advantage of *speech* for the communication of ideas, it is, in several respects, infinitely inferior to the art of *Writing*. Since by the one the power of communication is confined both in point of time and place, and in the other it is absolutely unconfined with respect to both. By words we

can

can converfe only with thofe who are prefent with us, but by means of writing we
become acquainted with the fentiments and
tranfactions of men in all ages, and all
nations of the world. It connects, as it
were, the living, the dead, and the unborn:
for, by writing, the prefent age can not
only receive information from the greateft
and the wifeft of mankind before them, but
are themfelves able to convey wifdom and
inftruction to the lateft pofterity.

But, notwithftanding the fuperiority of
writing to fpeaking in the abovementioned
refpects, it is but a fubftiute for the art of
fpeaking; and, where both can be ufed,
vaftly inferior to it. Not to mention the
eafe and readinefs of vocal expreffion, letters
can only exprefs the fimple founds of words,
without the particular tone and inflection of the voice with which they are fpoken:

on

on which, notwithstanding, very often, the most important part of the meaning depends: for, in conversation, we attend as much to the manner in which a thing is said, as to the words themselves. By the tone of the voice we can vary, and modify our ideas in a manner that no power of letters can ever equal. In *Irony* the meaning of words is quite reversed. In mentioning a person's name, or only the word *Sir*, we either simply call to him, or, in the strongest manner in the world, without any additional words, express our tenderness, respect, anger, contempt, reproach, and almost every other passion, and degree of passion, that the human mind is capable of.

The transition from speaking to writing is so far from being thought easy and natural by many persons, that some of the greatest men this nation ever produced, particularly

Sir

Sir *Isaac Newton*, and Dr. *Hartley*, have had recourfe to fupernatural interpofition to account for it, and fuppofe that the firft alphabetical writings were the two tables of ftone, which were written by the finger of God himfelf. And it muft be acknowledged, that the oldeft accounts we have concerning the ufe of letters in *Afia* and *Greece* is fo circumftanced, as by no means to clafh with their hypothefis. It feems likewife very probable, from *Robertfon*'s comparifon of Alphabets, that all the known ones might originally have been derived from the *Hebrew*, or *Samaritan*. They, moreover, alledge, that, to exprefs all the variety of articulations of which the human voice is capable, by fo few fimple characters, would, have appeared fo difficult a problem to the firft rude ages of mankind, that, had it ever been propofed to them, they could never have thought of attempting the folution of it.

But

But thefe gentlemen do not feem to have confidered, that though thofe rude fore-fathers of the human race might have been incapable of decyphering, and reducing into an Alphabet, all the articulations of the human voice, in its prefent extent; yet, neverthelefs, partly by chance (which hath been the mother of moft of our ufeful inventions) and partly by attention to the fubject, they might have hit upon a method of making a fort of alphabet for the comparatively few and fimple articulations that themfelves made ufe of; which might grow in perfection with the language it reprefented.

It muft likewife be confidered that the pronunciation of thofe rude ages, being ufed chiefly to exprefs very ftrong apprehenfions, muft have been peculiarly loud, and diftinct: befides, like children when they firft learn a language, or men who are not per-

C   fectly

fectly mafters of a new one, they would be obliged to fpeak very flow, both to favour the flownefs of their own inventions, and recollections, and alfo to make themfelves underftood by others who were not more per- fect in the ufe of language than themfelves. Thefe circumftances would afford them a much fairer opportunity of obferving the different pofition of the organs, and diftin- guifhing the feveral articulations of fpeech than the prefent method of pronunciation affords us.

Some pofitions of the organs attending articulation, one would think, they might foon diftinguifh; being vifible to the eye, as well as perceived in their effects by the ear, and felt in their own pronunciation: for inftance, the fhutting and different aper- ture of the lips, likewife the hiffing found of [s], that of [r], and feveral others which,

which are very diftinguifhable, it is probable
might have been taken notice of very early,
and have had characters appropriated to them
before the reft. And the greater opening of
the mouth, attending the primitive violent pronunciation, would render the action of all the
organs, in the whole bufinefs of articulation,
more vifible than our way of fpeaking admits of.

Granting that men might, for fome time,
diftinguifh no more than four or fix letters,
or, one for each of the claffes into which we
divide them at prefent; as *labials*, *dentals*,
linguals, *palatines*, *gutturals* and the like,
they might afterwards obferve a difference in
the articulations they had at firft referred
to one letter, and make a proportionable
variation of their character. In this gradual
manner might their characters multiply,
till at length they were fufficient to com-

pofe

pofe an ancient alphabet.   Some articulations feem to be fufficiently diftinguifhable
to have given a hint for a beginning, and a
beginning once made, the progrefs feems
not to have been very difficult.   And even
an imperfect apprehenfion of the ufe and
advantage of fuch an invention would quick-
en their endeavours to perfect it.

It feems to favour thefe obfervations,
that the *Eaftern*, which are the oldeft, alphabets have no vowels, the pofitions of the
organs of fpeech to exprefs the confonants
being very diftinguifhably different, it is natural to fuppofe they would invent characters
for them firft.   Whereas the vowels, being
produced by little more than different degrees
of the aperture of the mouth, they might
not think of diftinguifhing them by characters, till their alphabet was formed; when,
on account of their making ufe of it for the
notation

notation of numbers, and other similar pur-
poses, it might have been inconvenient to alter the form of it, so much as they must have
done to incorporate the vowels into it. They
therefore at first distinguished the vowels by
general custom, or general rules; and afterwards by other methods, which did not interfere with the consonants.

To these let me add another observation,
which is, that the imperfection of all alphabets, the *Hebrew* by no means excepted,
seems to argue them not to have been the
product of divine skill, but the result of
such a concurrence of accident and gradual
improvement as all human arts, and what
we call inventions, owe their birth to. For,
certainly, the alphabets in use bear no marks
of the regularity and perfection of the works
of nature: the more we consider the latter,
the more reason we see to admire their beau-

ty,

ty, juſt proportions, and conſequent fitneſs
to anſwer their reſpective ends; whereas,
the more we examine the former, the more
defects, ſuperfluities, and imperfections of
all kinds we diſcover in them. Beſides,
had there ever been a divine alphabet, it
would certainly have eſtabliſhed itſelf in the
world by its manifeſt excellence, particularly as, upon this ſuppoſition, mankind were
incapable of diviſing one themſelves.

LECTURE

LECTURE the THIRD.

OF

HIEROGLYPHICKS,

CHINESE CHARACTERS,

AND

DIFFERENT ALPHABETS.

NOTWITHSTANDING the probability of *Alphabetical writing* having been nothing more than a human invention, it seems to be too perfect a method of fixing and conveying our ideas to have been

the

the firſt that mankind would hit upon.
Indeed, both natural probability and hiſtory
ſhow that *picture-writing*, with the contraction
of it into *Hieroglyphics*, and the ſtill further
refinement of it into a character like the
Chineſe, was prior to it.   I ſhall briefly il-
luſtrate this method in all its gradations.

To give a diſtinct idea of the ſubject, let
it be obſerved, that, whereas *Alphabetical*
writing is the repreſentation of *words* as
ſounds, and can therefore be underſtood
only by perſons who uſe the ſame language,
the characters we are now conſidering are
the repreſentations or pictures of *things*
themſelves, without regard to the intervention of any ſounds whatever, and are
therefore equally intelligible to perſons
uſing any language.

To expreſs a tree, or animal, they who
firſt

firſt uſed this method would probably begin in the moſt ſimple manner, by drawing an actual ſketch or outline of the tree or animal, and proceed in like manner to depict all other viſible objects. To repreſent ſounds, they might draw the viſible circumſtances attending the production of it, which thoſe who have any notion of painting will eaſily conceive; and for ideas of things ſtill more remote from ſight, they might have recourſe to *analogies*, or *metaphors* drawn from ſenſible things; thus *eternity* was depicted by a *ſerpent biting its tail; impoſſibility*, by *two feet ſtanding upon water*, &c.

By degrees they would learn to contract theſe pictures, and only to draw ſo much of their firſt outline as was ſufficient to diſtinguiſh one expreſſion from another. Thus *two ſwords*, and then *two croſs-ſtrokes* would ſerve to expreſs a *battle;* which was

at

at firft reprefented by the figures of men in a fighting pofture; and to denote impoffibility, a plain horizontal line might fuffice for the water, and two upright ftrokes for feet, &c. In a medium between *picture-writing* and the laft contractions of them we fhould probably find the *Hieroglyphical* writing of the ancient *Egyptians*, and the laft contraction of this picture or analogical writing (intermixed with a great number of arbitrary characters, to reprefent ideas and not words) may conftitute the writing of the *Chinefe;* which is faid to be underftood by feveral nations inhabiting the eaftern parts of *Afia*, though they fpeak different languages.

The laft improvement of fuch a method as this may be illuftrated by the characters that we ourfelves ufe to denote numbers. 1. 2. 3. &c. and the character &. Thefe are arbitrary marks, to denote ideas directly, without

without the intervention of words, and are alike known to all the nations of *Europe*. Imagine now that not only the ideas of numbers, and the particle *and* but all our other ideas and particles were denoted in the fame manner, by arbitrary characters, which any nation might ufe, at the fame time that they gave them what names they pleafed, and we fhould have the ideas of juft fuch a written language as the *Chinefe* is faid to be.

A few arbitrary characters, to reprefent ideas directly, as the *nine digits* &c. we find to be extremely ufeful, and preferable to any other method of expreffing the fame things; but it is eafy to fee, that this me-thod, extended to all our ideas, would in-creafe our written characters to a moft enor-mous and unmanagable quantity: and we are told that it is, in fact, the bufinefs of half the life of a *Chinefe* philofopher to

learn

learn barely to read a sufficient variety of books in their language: and the difficulty of inventing, and establishing the use of new characters (without which they could have no way of expressing new ideas) must itself prevent the growth of arts and sciences in that nation. This being considered, we need not wonder that, contrary to what hath happened in other nations, arts and sciences should have been so early invented by those people, and yet have been at a stand for upwards of a thousand years: and till they remove this impediment, and introduce *alphabetical writing*, it is no difficult matter to foresee, that they never can make much greater progress than they have already made in the sciences, and that all the improvements they will henceforward receive they must derive from *European* philosophers, and *European* languages.

The

The moft ancient *Alphabets* that we are acquainted with are certainly thofe which are adapted to the *Eaftern* tongues: and indeed, from the *Eaft*, both letters, and the firft feeds of all the fciences were brought into Europe. The derivation of the *Greek alphabet* from the *Hebrew*, *Samaritan*, or *Syriac* (which it is probable, were all of them, originally, the fame with the *Phenician*) is very evident; and the letters do very much refemble them in fhape, confidering the changes that, either chance, or defign, would neceffarily, in a courfe of time, bring into a thing of fuch a nature.

But what is a much ftronger proof is hiftorical evidences, which with one voice attribute the introduction of letters into *Greece*, to the *Pelafgi* in the firft place, who alfo afterwards carried them into *Italy*, and then to one *Cadmus*, who brought them

D from

from *Phenicia*, Befides the very order of the letters in the *Greek* alphabet, demon-ftrates the fame thing, by its correfpondence with that of the *Hebrew*, excepting thofe chafms which were made by the *Greeks* not adopting fuch *Hebrew* letters as they had no founds anfwering to; which chafms were in part filled up by others, fome of which *Palamedes* about the fiege of *Troy*, and the reft *Simonides*, fome time after, are faid to have invented.

The ancient *Latin* Alphabet was nearly the fame with the *Greek*, before the laft additions were made to it, retaining the F of the *Æolians* (when the reft of *Greece* had rejected it) and the ufe which the *Pelafgi* and ancient *Greeks* made of the H, which was an afpirate.

Moreover, the *Greeks* univerfally (after
the

the *Bæotians*, who firſt borrowed the practice) denoted all their *numbers* by the very
ſame letters which the *Hebrews* made uſe
of to denote them.   And, to make their
Alphabet tally with the *Hebrew* for this
purpoſe, they filled up all the remaining
chaſms in their old Alphabet with real *Hebrew* letters; of which they made no other
uſe than as *numerals;* calling them, by way
of diſtinction

It is, further, probable that the ancient
Greeks, in imitation of the *Phenicians*,
wrote from the right hand to the left; that
afterwards they wrote alternately from the
right to the left, and from the left to
the right, always beginning the next line
where they ended the preceding; which way
of writing they called   *,*
from the reſemblance it bore to the manner
of driving oxen in plowing, (ſome ſpecimens

of

of which yet remain) before it was fixed
in the method in which, at length, they, and
after them, all the nations of *Europe* have
ufed it; viz. from the left hand to the right,
without variation. All the *Eaftern* nations,
whofe language is alphabetical, except the
Armenians, write from the right hand to
the left; though the *Chinefe, Japanefe,*
and others, whofe language is not alphabetical, write in neither of the abovementioned
directions.

Though the alphabets at prefent in ufe
among the *Arabians, Perfians,* and
Æthiopians, have no great analogy to the
Hebrew or *Syriac,* either in the number or
order of the letters, (and the *Æthiopic*
language, contrary to them all, is written,
like *European* languages, from the left
hand to the right) the moft ancient
alphabets

alphabets of all thofe people differ very little from it; in fo much that there is fufficient
reafon to believe, they had all one origin.(*a*)
The fubfequent alterations were eafy to
make, when the method of writing alphabe-
tically was once invented, as we fee a
variety of *fhort-hands* are daily contrived by
ourfelves. *(b)*

D 3   The

(*a*) Sir *Ifaac Newton* fuppofes that the *Edom-
ites* were very early acquainted with letters, as
well as Navigation, Aftronomy, and other arts
and fciences; and that from them *Mofes* learned
to write the law in a book.

(*b*) The *Gothic* characters invented by *Ulfilas*
about the year of our lord 370, were in ufe in
moft parts of *Europe* after the deftruction of the
Weftern Empire.   The *French* firft admitted the
Latin character.   The *Spaniards* by decree of a
fynod at *Lyons* abolifhed the ufe of the *Gothic*
character A. D. 1091.

The notation of founds differs remarkably in the manner in which *vowels* are expreſſed in different languages. No *Eaſtern* language had originally any characters for vowels, and their alphabets to this day conſiſt only of conſonants. Afterwards, to fix the pronunciation, which oral inſtruction muſt have determined before, little marks were invented, and placed either above or below the letters, to ſupply the place of vowels. The *Ethiopians*, inſtead of making vowel points diſtinct from the conſonants, affix a kind of *dot* to a particular part of the letter to expreſs the vowel accompanying it. But as theſe dots are affixed according to certain rules, and alter not the ſound of the conſonant to which they are annexed, though they make a ſmall alteration in the character, they ought not to be conſidered as adding to the number of the letters of their alphabet. This however

ever

ever fome have admitted, and by this means have increafed the *Ethiopic* alphabet from 26, to 202 letters.

All *European* nations make diftinct cha-racters for vowels, and, from the analogy between the ancient *Greek* and prefent *Hebrew* Alphabet, there are fome who think it not improbable but anciently were the vowels a. e. i. o. u. refpectivly, and not confidered as confonants, upon the fame rank with the reft.

It is a great inconvenience attending the orthography of all modern languages, that the pronunciation doth not correfpond with the writing, but that the fame letters have different founds, and the fame founds are often expreffed by different letters: fome letters alfo, according to the pronunciation, are

are fuperfluous in fome words, in others letters are wanting. This is chiefly a mark
of their derivation from other languages:
fince, in many of thofe differences, the fpel-
ling leans to the ancients, when the pronunciation is modern. Thus the *(p)* in the
word *receipt* is not pronounced; but it fhews
the derivation of the word from *recipio* in
Latin. Some words of the fame found are
fpelled differently, to preferve a diftinction
in writing, as *air* to breath, from *heir* of an
eftate. Other words, on the contrary, which
are fpelled in the fame manner, are pronounced differently, to preferve a diftinction
in fpeaking; as I *read*, and I have *read*.
There would be no foundation for feveral
of thefe differences in a primitive language:
for, fince the original ufe of written characters was fimply to exprefs the very founds
men actually ufed, they muft, at leaft as
near as they could, have been made to
correfpond with the pronunciation.

The

The Alphabets of all Languages were for many ages fingle, the diftinction of letters into *Capitals* and *fmall-letters* being, comparatively, of late contrivance. In general, the letters that we ufe as capitals were the common and only characters of the *Greeks* and *Romans,* the fmall letters being a contraction of them for the fake of expedition. Several nations of the *Eaft* have different fets of letters, and fome which they always write larger than others; yet they do not ufe them as we do our *capitals,* to diftinguifh particular words, by placing them fingle at their head, but for the *titles of books,* or whole books for particular ufes. In moft *Eaftern* languages, letters, for the convenience of joining, are fhaped differently, according as they are to be placed at the beginning, the middle, or the end of a word.

Characters were not ufed originally to exprefs

exprefs any thing befides *words*. Characters
to denote *paufes*, and feveral affections of
the fenfe are of late invention, for the *Ancients* wrote the words of a fentence contiguous, with fewer intervals than are made
in pronouncing them; as appears by ancient
manufcripts. It is faid that characters to
exprefs paufes were invented about the year
of Chrift 360; but at firft they made ufe of
nothing but dots for that purpofe: the different pofition of them expreffing the different length of the paufes: by degrees different marks were introduced, and at length
different affections of the fenfe were noted
by characters, to make the meaning more
eafily apprehended: of this nature are the
notes of interrogation, and exclamation,
placed at the clofe of a fentence.

All modern *European* languages, and
Latin are pointed in the fame manner.
The

The *Greek* is pointed with some variation, the *Semicolon* in other languages becoming the note of interrogation in that. In *Greek* there is also only one pause intermediate between the *comma* and the *period,* and it is a single dot placed at the top of the line.

The *Hebrew* hath thirty two accents, which also serve to denote pauses; but, according to *Capellus* they were only invented by the *Mazorites* about the year 400 after Christ.

Characters are also used various other ways to direct the pronunciation of words. Some are called *accents,* and formerly shewed when to raise or depress the voice, without lengthening or shortening the sylla- ble. In modern languages accents con- found both; for the syllable that is ac- cented is pronounced stronger, if not upon

a higher key, and at the fame time length-
ened. Chara&ters are alfo ufed to fhew the
omiffion of letters in words and various
other purpofes. They are liable to frequent innovations.

LECTURE

LECTURE the FOURTH.

OF THE

GENERAL DISTRIBUTION

OF WORDS

INTO CLASSES.

IN order to give a clear account of the principles of Language and Grammar, we muſt endeavour to trace the uſe of words to their origin, and through the whole courſe

E   of

of their progrefs; from their firft rude ftate, to their laft refinements.

It is natural to fuppofe that the firft words which mankind, in the moft early ages of the world, would invent and apply, would be names for fenfible objects; as of animals, vegetables, the parts of the human body, the fun, moon, &c. becaufe thefe are the things that would firft occur to their obfervation, and which their neceffities would oblige them to have the moft conftant recourfe to. Thefe names conftitute the firft, and moft important clafs of words, under the Grammatical appellation of NOUNS SUBSTANTIVE. The names of individuals would be proper and incommunicable, as *Adam, Eve, Paradice,* &c. other names would be applied, by analogy, to every other of the fame fpecies, and conftitute the general names of *men, tree, river, garden,* &c.

After

After obferving things *in the grofs*, men would attend to their parts and properties; and finding in many of them properties which they had in common with others; as *hardnefs, foftnefs, length, breadth, white-nefs, rednefs*, &c. they would get names for fenfible, and other qualities, which would not belong to any one object or fpe-cies of objects in particular, but, upon be-ing named, would recall to their minds ideas of a variety of things indifferently. Thefe properties or qualities, confidered in them-felves, abftracted from any fubject to which they belong, convey to our minds certain determinate ideas, and therefore the names of them are nouns of the fame clafs with thofe abovementioned; but confidered as exifting in, and infeparable from the parti-cular fubjects to which they belonged, it would be found convenient to refine upon the language, and give the preceding words

E 2 another

another form.   Thus a *lion,* inftead of being called a beaft of ftrength, would be
called *ftrong.*   The name of a quality in
this form is called an ADJECTIVE.   It is
obfervable that the *Hebrew* and other very
ancient and fimple languages have few adjectives. *(a)*   Indeed, as they exprefs the
fame ideas with their correfponding fubftantives,   only more conveniently modified for
feveral particular ufes,   they are not abfolutely neceffary for the purpofes of fpeech.

As properties or qualities of things, when
ufed

(a) Thus St. *Paul,* following the *Hebrew*
idiom, fays 2 Cor. iv. 6. *The light of the know-*
ledge of the glory of GOD; when adjectives, in a
language that abounded with them, might have
been introduced with advantage, and have given
the expreffion the following more intelligible
turn, *The enlightening knowledge of the glorious*
GOD.

used in the form of adjectives, imply some subject to which they belong, they form no determinate idea without their substantives, and are therefore always used in conjunction with them: for example, when I say *strong*, I do not mean strength in general; which would suggest an abstract idea, capable of being the subject of a proposition or argumentation; but some particular thing that hath strength: the mind is therefore in suspence, till I name something in conjunction with it, as *strong man*, *strong horse*, &c.

In using a name that is common to a whole species we may either intend to speak of some of the species in general, or of one or more than one in particular. To mark this difference, some languages prefix to nouns words which, because of their importance, they distinguish by a particular name, viz.

E 3   ARTICLES:

ARTICLES: the article *indefinite* in the former cafe and the article *definite* in the latter. In *Englifh (a)* is ufed for the former, and *the* for the latter. Thus *a man* is any one man indifferently; whereas *the man* means fome particular man, either mentioned before, or fo circumftanced as not to be miftaken.

Articles are neceffarily of the nature of adjectives, as they always imply fome fub-ftantive to which they belong, which they characterize, and when named without them leave the mind under the fame kind of fuf-penfc. The fame characters are alfo found to belong to the words *this, that, every,* and the like; which fome Grammarians call articles, and others pronouns. Grammarians who make articles a part of fpeech dif-tinct from adjectives define them to be *words which fix or limit the fignification of nouns,* which

which is true of all adjectives whatever.
For do not the words *great*, *small*, *wife*,
all, *every*, &c. and, in like manner, every
other adjective fix, limit, or ascertain the
signification of nouns, which, without such
words, would be more unrestrained and in-
determinate. *(a)*

As the sole use of speech is mutual information, men would never have occasion
to name any object but to affirm something
concerning it: their first efforts in speech
                                    therefore

(a) Even when a natural property of a thing
is expressed by an adjective, we, as it were, limit
and confine the attention to that particular con-
sideration of it : for instance, when we say *mortal men*, we mean men, not considered univer-
sally, but as mortal only : and unless the nature
of the discourse require that we view the substantive in that particular light, it is an impropriety
in style to mention that epithet.

therefore would be to form a propofition. A *propofition*, accurately fpeaking, is a fentence which expreffes the agreement or coincidence of two ideas. To exprefs this agreement or coincidence, men would probably, at firft, only name them one after the other; as children do when they firft learn to fpeak: for example, they would fay *a lion ftrength*, or *a lion ftrong*, inftead of faying *a lion hath ftrength*, or *a lion is ftrong:* it would foon, however, be found convenient to introduce fome word to denote this affirmation. This word which fimply expreffes the affirmation, or fignifies the agreement between two ideas is called *the verb fubftantive*, and every word that is called a verb includes it.

Every fentence that contains an affirmation muft, neceffarily, contain three ideas; namely two of nouns, the agreement of

which

which is expreffed, and one of the verb
fubftantive, which denotes their agreement;
though the terms may be fo contrived, as
that one of them fhall imply any two of the
ideas, or all the three.   For example, in
the fentence *He is ftanding*, the two ex-
treme terms are both nouns, or names, the
word *he* being a fubftitute for the name of
fome particular perfon; and the word *ftand-*
ing the name of a particular pofture.   The
fentence affirms that the pofture of the perfon referred to by the word *he*, and that
which anfwers to the word *ftanding* are the
fame; and the verb *is* expreffes this famenefs or agreement: but the nature of the
Latin language is fuch, that any two, or
all of thefe ideas may be reprefented by one
term.   *Ille eft ftans* contains them all feparate: in *Eft ftans* the two former are united:
in *Ille ftat* the two latter: and in *ftat* all
the

the three. Our own language admits of the union of the two laſt as *He ſtands*.

Every word which, when analized, is found to contain the idea of the ſimple affirmation is called a VERB. To define it ſtrictly and univerſally. A *Verb* either expreſſes the ſimple affirmation only, or the ſimple affirmation joined with the name of the ſtate or condition of the ſubject concerning which the affirmation is made; which ſubject alſo, in ſome languages, and in ſome circumſtances, is likewiſe comprehended in it.

This general definition eaſily comprehends all kinds of verbs, whether *active, paſſive, or neuter*. Thus in the ſentence *Pompeius pugnat, Pompey is fighting*, the verb *pugnat* implies both the ſimple affirmation, and the name of the ſtate or condition

tion that Pompey is faid to be in, namely
fighting. In *Pompeius occiditur, Pompey
is killed;* the verb *occiditur* implies the
fame, namely the fimple affirmation, and
the ftate or condition of the fubject of it,
flain. Laftly, in *Pompeius requiefcit* the
verb implies both the affirmation and the
ftate of *reft.*

Befides the coincidence, or agreement of
ideas, the purpofe of thinking and fpeaking
requires that other affections or relations of
them be attended to. Thefe are expreffed
in different manners in different languages.
I fhall illuftrate this by one relation; namely
that of caufe and effect; fpeaking of the
divine being and of the world, and intend-
ing to exprefs the former to be the caufe of
the latter, we fhould, in *English,* put the
word (of) between them, and fay *the
creator of the world.* In *Latin* the termination

nation of the latter undergoes an alteration, as *creator mundi*. In *Hebrew* the alteration takes place in the former.

Words appropriated to denote the relations of nouns to a part, or the whole of the sentence are called PREPOSITIONS. They abound in all languages: for it would create endless confusion to vary the termination of words for every different relation. Even in *Greek* and *Latin*, only the principal, and more usual relations of words are expressed by a change of termination.

Among the last orders of words I shall mention those which are substitutes for other words,

CONJUNCTIONS are words which connect sentences together, and express their relation to one another: but they are not absolutely

absolutely neceſſary to ſpeech; becauſe, in
all caſes, the ſentences which they connect
may be thrown into one; and the only advantage of them is, that they give an eaſier
turn to an expreſſion which would otherwiſe
be perplexed and aukward. For example,
I can either ſay, in one formal ſentence;
His command was the reaſon of my writing;
or, more elegantly, in two, with a conjunction, *I wrote becauſe he ordered me.* The
word *becauſe* connects theſe two ſentences,
which are formed out of one, and ſhews
the relation they bear to one another; which
is that of *cauſe and effect.*

In like manner, there are no conjunctions
whatever but what may be ſaid to ſupply the
place of other words; ſince they only change
the form of expreſſing the ſame things.
Even the ſimple conjunction *and,* ſtrictly
ſpeaking, is not neceſſary. We may either

F ſay,

say, *Cæsar conquered Gaul, and enslaved his country;* or, *Cæsar conquered Gaul: Cæsar enslaved his country.* In this sentence, the use of the conjunction is to supercede the necessity of repeating the subject of the proposition. In the sentence, *Alexander and Cæsar were great conquerors,* the conjunction serves instead of repeating what Logicians call the predicate of the proposition. If it be said that the conjunction is still understood, though the sentence be resolved into two, and that we ought to say, *Alexander was a great conqueror, and Cæsar was a great conqueror;* it is evident that the word *and* is nothing more than a contraction for *I, with the same truth, affirm;* or some such periphrasis.

This class of words, therefore, must be ranked rather among the elegancies than the necessaries of a language; though they are

so

so nearly neceffary, that they claim the firft place among thofe that are not fo.

To avoid the repetition of names of very frequent occurrence, all nations have found the convenience of ufing fhorter words in their place, or general terms inftead of particular, when the difcourfe was fo circumftanced as to prevent any miftake of the particulars referred to. For example, inftead of laying every fpeaker under the neceffity of repeating his own name every time he mentioned his having done any thing, or that of the perfon he was fpeaking to whenever he addreffed him, we ufe *I* in the former cafe, and *thou* in the latter; which are made univerfal terms, being equally applicable to every perfon who fpeaks, and every perfon who is fpoken to. Alfo, inftead of naming any perfon or thing very often, after having ufed the proper name once, we

F 2 afterwards

afterwards content ourselves with using the words *He, she, it,* &c. instead of it. These words are termed Pronouns, being used instead of nouns.

The words called Adverbs are also contractions for other words, or rather clusters of words, as *here,* for *in this place; there, in that place; wisely, in a wise manner; dayly, every day,* &c. *(a)*

The

(a) It would likewise contribute greatly to the ease and distinctness of our conceptions, if we were to consider many other words and modifications of words, as substitutes for different words, and contractions of more complex expressions. For instance, the *imperative mood* of verbs may be considered as a contracted form of expressing a sentence, which would, in more words, indicate the command of the speaker to the hearer. Thus *scribe,* write thou, is equivalent to *jubeo ut scribas,* I command thee to write. Also when we interrogate as *scribisne?* dost thou write? it is

The words ufually known by the name of INTERJECTIONS are more properly the inarticulate expreffions of the paffions of *joy, forrow, anger, furprize,* and the like, than appropriated to any particular and determinate ideas. They are, accordingly, obferved to refemble the inarticulate founds of brute animals.

To give a brief fummary of this lecture. All the words of which the languages of men confift are either the names of things and qualities (the ideas of which exift in the mind) or words adapted to denote the relati-

F 3   ons

the fame thing as if we faid in more words, *I afk whether you be writing?* This analyfis of the more complex parts of fpeech makes our general definitions of words more diftinct, and prevents them from interfering with one another.

ons they bear to one another; or laftly, a compendium for other words, with or without their relations. The names of things or qualities are termed *Subftantives* and *Adjectives :* the fubftitutes of thefe are *Pronouns.* Their coincidence or agreement is expreffed by *Verbs :* The relations of words by *Prepofitions*, and of fentences by *Conjunctions.* And *Adverbs* are contracted forms of fpeech, which may be analized into words belonging to other claffes.

Having given a general view of the diftribution of words into claffes, I fhall confider each of the claffes more particularly.

LECTURE

LECTURE the FIFTH.

OF

NOUNS.

OF the kinds of words above enume-
rated, some may be considered in
different respects, as they are capable of
different affections: for example, in names
of things or *nouns*, we may consider their
number, sex, &c. The names of qualities or
adjectives admit of the degrees of more or less:
In *verbs* we may consider the person, the time
and other circumstances, of an affirmation.
Thefe

These affections are, in some languages, denoted by different modifications of the word, as by a change of termination. &c. in which languages these words are said to be *declinable*, in other languages these different affections are expressed by other additional words, or by their position only.

With respect to *substantives*, some of them are names of one particular person or thing; as *Athens*, a particular town; *Alexander*, a particular man; *Danube* a particular river.   Others are common to a whole species, as *town, man, river*.   In considering nouns of this latter kind, the first thing that occurs to us is, that we may intend to speak of one only, or of more of the species to which that name is common.   It hath been found convenient, therefore, I believe, in almost all languages, to use a different modification of the term when we
intend

intend to exprefs one only, or more of the kind; thus *homo* is one man only, *homines* more men than one. *(a)* The one is called the *Singular*, and the other *Plural* NUMBER.

As number is infinite, few nations have thought of diftinguifhing any particular number of things more than one by modifications of the term, but do it by diftinct words, exprefling the particular number intended: for example, there is no other method of exprefling *three men* in Latin than by faying *tres homines.* Though, with refpect to things which nature hath formed in pairs, and fometimes even things not connected in that manner, fome nations have contrived a particular modification
called

(a) In the *Peruvian* tongue, *Reland* fays, the plural number is exprefled, not by a change of the verbal termination, but by the addition of certain particles.

called the *Dual* number to exprefs them.
In Greek   is a hand,
two hands, and   any indefinite
number of hands.

But this modification is intirely fuperfluous: and even when, in particular cafes,
there is no provifion in a language to exprefs
the different numbers of Singular and
Plural, the inconvenience is not perceived,
if any other words in the fentence mark the
diftinction. In *Englifh*, though we fay *a
fheep feeds*, and *fheep feed*, and the word
fheep, to which the number properly belongs, have no modification to exprefs it by,
yet, as it is plainly pointed out by the words
it is connected with, the fentence is fufficiently free from ambiguity.

What we may call the caprice of all languages hath expreffed many things which
are

are really fingular by a plural termination,
as *bellows* in Englifh, and *caftra* in Latin.
In conftruction, the words connected with
them muft conform to the cafual termination, and not follow the fenfe; as *the bellows blow*, not *blows;* caftra *ponuntur*
not *ponitur.(a)*

In many languages nouns are differently
modified according to the different fex,
namely, male or female, which they either
really are of, or that is arbitrarily afcribed
to them. The male conftitutes the *Mafculine*,
and the female the *Feminine* GENDER. In
others a third clafs is made of thofe which are
of neither fex and is termed *neuter.* Other
languages,

(a) Though in *Hebrew* it be often otherwife
                    Sapientiæ clamat
as   *and the* LORD *fpake*

languages, particularly the *English, (b)* make no difference in the termination, but when there is a real difference of fex; and even this real difference is not always expreffed by a change of termination, but by words total-ly different. Thus *lion* is the male, and *lionefs* the female; but the female corref-ponding to a *horfe* is termed a *mare.* Indeed in languages in which the difference of fex is moft fcrupuloufly attended to, different words are appropriated to them where the difference is very ftriking; as *vir* a man, *mulier* a woman.

With refpect to fex, the *English* Lan-guage feems to have followed nature, and other languages, by aiming at two great refinement

(b) Of modern European languages, the *Ger-man* and the *Lapland* (and perhaps fome others) have neuters.

refinement, have departed from it, without gaining any advantage, which can be called an equivalent, for the abfurdity and additional intricacy attending the practice. Why is *lapis* mafculine, when *rupes* is feminine, and *faxum* neuter?

Befides the affections of number and fex, there are few languages but exprefs fome of the principal relations of one word to another by a further change of termination, or fome other modification. In *Latin* and *Greek* fix of the principal circumftances in which nouns are ufed are expreffed by a change of termination: they are called CASES and are the *Nominative*, *Genitive*, *Dative*, *Accufative*, *Vocative*, and *Ablative*. By the addition of prepofitions to fome particular cafes of words, they exprefs the remaining circumftances and relations. The application of thefe cafes is by no means

G

made

made with fufficient judgment, fince very different relations are expreffed promifcu-oufly by the fame cafe, and the fame relation by different cafes.

The ufe of the cafes in the *Greek* and *Latin* languages may perhaps be defined in the following general manner.

The *Nominative* is the cafe in which a thing is barely named, with refpect to fome fubfequent affirmation; as *fol ortus eft, the fun is rifen.*

The *Genitive* denotes property or poffef-fion; or that to which the thing it is connected with belongs, as *filius Pompeii, the fon of Pompey.* Q. Whofe fon is he? A. Pompey's. In like manner, *pater Pompeii,* the father of Pompey. Q. Whofe father

father is he?   A. Pompey's. *(a)*

This very general use of the *Genitive,* which comprehends in it, as some say, thirteen different relations, hath occasioned an ambiguity in some expressions where it occurs.   Thus *amor dei* may either signify the love that God bears to man, or the love that man bears to God; because, according to either of the two senses, the question suggested by the definition, to try the propriety of it's application, admits of a direct answer.   Q. Whose is this love?   A. God's. either as the object, or the subject of it.

C 2   The

(a) The remains of some of the *Saxon* genitives which ended in *es,* are preserved in the apostrophe and *s* in *English;* as *Solomon's wisdom;* in *Chaucer's* time, the *e* and consequent additional syllable were in use; as *Goddes folk,* *God's folk,* or *God's people.*

The *Dative* cafe characterizes the perfon or thing to which another that it is connected with is given, attributed, or afcribed; as *do librum puero*, I give a book to the boy. Q. To whom do I give it? A. To the boy.

This definition of the *Dative* interfering in fome circumftances with the Genitive is the reafon why, in thofe inftances, the cafes are ufed promifcuoufly; as *filius Pompeii*, or *filius Pompeio*. For fince, in the firft inftance, Pompey anfwering to the queftion, whofe fon is he? determines its right to be put in the genitive cafe; its equally anfwering to the queftion to whom is he attributed, or afcribed, viz. as a fon? doth likewife declare its right to the Dative, according to fuch definitions as muft be made to comprehend all the relations thofe

cafes

cases are used to express. *(a)*

The *Accusative* denotes the person or thing on which the action of a verb transi-ive passeth; as *Cæsar vicit Pompeum,* Cæsar conquered Pompey. Whom did Cæsar conquer? A. Pompey.

The *Vocative* is only used in calling to a person: as this case is of very little use, it is generally the same with the nominative.

The *Ablative* is made use of to express

G 3

many

(a) Mr. *Harris* defines the *Genitive* to be a case which is formed to express all relations com-mencing from itself; and the *Dative* to express all relations tending to itself. The observation is ingenious, and generally just: but it seems to be too philosophical for so vague and irregular an use as is actually made of those cases. In particular, there is, in this description, no pro-vision for the promiscuous use of them : for how can any word be in a relation which may be con-sidered indifferently either as commencing from itself, or tending to itself?

many other relations of words to words, in conjunction with prepofitions, appropriated to the particular relations; as *in horto*, *in the garden : cum exercitu*, with an army. When no prepofition accompanies it, it generally denotes the inftrument wherewith a thing is done; as *gladio*, with a fword. The *Accufative* alfo and, in Greek, the *Genitive* and *Dative* too, are ufed in conjunction with prepofitions to denote other relations than thofe which they exprefs when alone.

In *Englifh*, and moft other modern languages, prepofitions are ufed without any change of cafe, to anfwer the purpofes of the *Genitive*, *Dative*, and *Ablative*: and what the Latins and Greeks diftinguifhed by the *Accufative* cafe, we diftinguifh by its place after the verb, when the fenfe will not fuffice to determine it; as, *Alexander vicit Darium,*

Darium, Alexander conquered Darius.(a)

It is obfervable, as was hinted at before, that in *Hebrew*, to exprefs that which makes the Genitive in *Latin* and *Greek*, the alteration doth not affect the fame word that undergoes the change of termination in thofe languages, but the word which in them remains unchanged. For example in *verba regis, the words of the king*, the latter word hath been changed from *rex* ; whereas, to exprefs the fame thing in *Hebrew*, we muft fay   in which the former hath been changed from

The

(a) The cafes of nouns in the *Welch* language are expreffed by a change of the initial letters, if they be of thofe that are mutable, according to the prepofition or word that governs them. E. G. *ty* is a houfe; *dodrefn fy nhy* is the furniture of my houfe; *iw dy*, to his houfe; *prynodd dy*, he bought a houfe; and *allan o'i thy*, out of her houfe.

The *Hebrew,* and other *Eastern* tongues have this further peculiarity, that in them nouns undergo another change of termination, according to the perſon or perſons to whom the thing they ſpeak of belongs, or according to the pronouns poſſeſſive which, in other languages, are joined with them. For example, *my word;* which in *Latin* is *verbum meum,* in Hebrew is from   a word, and this occaſions a prodigious variety of terminations in their nouns. In reality, theſe pronominal terminations are the pronouns poſſeſſive contracted, and affixed to the nouns; from whence they have obtained the name of affixes.*(a)*

There

(a) There is ſomething analogous to this in the *Welch* language; in that it hath thirteen pronouns affixed to propoſitions, as *at, to, attaf,* to me ; *attal,* to thee, *atto,* to him.

There are few languages in which fub-ftantives do not fometimes become *Diminu-tives*, by a change of termination, that is, when we would exprefs fomething lefs than the ufual natural fize, we have not al-ways recourfe to an adjective, expreffing the degree of diminution; but change the word itfelf for that purpofe: thus *rivus* a river, becomes *rivulus*, a rivulet.   The *Italian* tongue not only abounds in Diminutives, but alfo in *Augmentatives* which exprefs fomething exceeding the natural fize, as from *capello* a hat, comes *capellone* a great hat, *capellacio* a great ugly hat.   They are not quite unknown in other languages.

ECTURE

LECTURE the SIXTH.

OF

ADJECTIVES

AND

PRONOUNS.

ADJECTIVES, on account of their connection with Subftantives, as they always fuppofe, and refer to them, have in fome languages, all the modifications of fubftantives; being declined with number,

number, cafe, and gender. *(a)* Whereas
in other languages, (fince the diftinctions of
number, cafe, and gender, are fufficiently
marked by the fubftantives) adjectives are
ufed without any variation in thofe refpects.
Thus in the expreffion *good men,* it is fufficiently evident, from the form of the
word *men,* that more than one are meant;
and

(a) In languages that admit of a change of
termination on account of gender, men and women cannot, in many cafes, ufe the fame form
of expreffion promifcuoufly. E. G. In *Latin* a
man fays *ego fum liber,* a woman, *ego fum libera.*
But it is remarkable that, in fome of the *Caribbee
Iflands,* the men and women hardly call any
thing by the fame name. This *Reland* conjec-
tures to have taken its rife from the conqueft of
the iflands, by a people who fpoke a language
different from that of the old inhabitants: in
confequence of which the men were expelled,
but the women ftayed with the conquerors; and,
retaining their own tongue, taught a great part
of it to their daughters.

and therefore that any alteration in the word *good* would be unneceſſary.

But as adjectives denote the qualities or properties of things, and theſe are eaſily perceived to admit of the degrees *more and leſs;* in moſt languages, theſe degrees are expreſſed by different modifications of the word. For example, *durus* is *hard,* the quality in general; *durior, harder,* the quality increaſed; and *duriſſimus, hardeſt,* or poſſeſſing the quality in the higheſt degree. In ſome languages the term is farther varied to expreſs a very ſmall degree of a quality, as *whitiſh, a little white.*

But in *Hebrew, French,* and ſome other languages, theſe different degrees of quality are expreſſed, not by any change of termination, but by other words appropriated to that purpoſe; as *ſage,* wiſe; *plus ſage, wiſer;*

wifer; le plus fage, wifeft. The *Hebrew*, in order to exprefs a very great degree of a quality, repeat the fimple expreffion of it; as *good, good;* that is *very good.* (*a*)

This comparifon of adjectives is founded on the fame principle with the Diminutives, and Augmentatives of fubftantives; but as the variation of degree is more eafily perceived, and oftener ufed in adjectives, the comparifon of adjectives hath become more general.

H   ARTICLES

(*a*) The *Welch,* befides the three degrees of comparifon, common to other languages, hath a fort of comparifon which imports, fometimes *equality,* and fometimes *admiration:* it is formed by adding *ed* to the pofitive; as *glan,* fair; *Cyn laned ac yntef,* as fair as he; *glaned yw,* how fair he is.

ARTICLES, being ufed in the fame manner as adjectives, are, in all languages, inflected as other adjectives are. They are not indeed compared; but neither do many other adjectives admit of comparifon, as *omnis all,* and many others.

In languages that have only one article, it is generally definite; the word itfelf without the article being then ufed in the indefinite fenfe. Thus in *Englifh,* which has no article indefinite in the plural number, *men* means any men; and *the men,* fome particular men: in the fame manner as *a man* means any man, and *the man* fome particular man.

Of PRONOUNS.

PRONOUNS, being nothing more than commodious fubftitutes for nouns, are not entitled to a diftinct clafs among the different kinds of words; but might all of them have been ranked under the heads of fubftantives, or adjectives; only the univerfal irregularity of their inflexions makes it neceffary to give them a diftinct confideration.

Pronouns are words of fuch frequent occurrence, that even in thofe languages which admit of few modifications of other words, feveral are, in a manner, obliged, for the greater eafe and certainty of diftinction, to be introduced here. Thus the *Englifh*, and *French*, who do not decline nouns with cafes, have feveral cafes for

H 2　　　　　　　fome

some of their pronouns as *Je, moi, me;
I, me; thou, thee; who, whom, whose.(a)*

Pronouns are either barely substitutes
for proper names of persons, and are therefore themselves substantives, or for persons
and things in particular circumstances. The
first are distinguished by the name of *per-
sonal* pronouns; and the rest by several other
denominations; according to the various
circumstances in which the person or thing
they relate to is considered, as *Possessive,
Relative,* and *Demonstrative.*

Ego, I, which is an universal substitute
for the person who speaks, is termed *the
first person. Tu, thou,* standing for the
name

(a) The *Teutonic* language, and that dialect
of it the *Saxon,* from which the present *English*
is derived, hath a dual number in their pronouns.

name of the perſon ſpoken to, *the ſecond*
perſon; and *Ille, he,* the perſon ſpoken of,
the third perſon. Their plurals *We, Ye,*
They, ſtand in the ſame order. *(a)*

H 3 I

(a) It is very entertaining to obſerve how differently the perſonal pronouns are applied, in the
complimental language of different nations.
Ancient languages, and thoſe of people who pretend to no politeneſs, admit of no other than
the ſecond perſon ſingular when we addreſs any
ſingle perſon; as *if thou pleaſe,* or, *if it pleaſe thee.*
The *Engliſh* and *French* uſe the ſecond perſon
plural; as *ſ'il vous plait, if you pleaſe.* The *Spa-*
niards uſe the third perſon ſingular; as *if he*
pleaſe; and the *Germans* the third perſon plural,
if they pleaſe. In the *Singalian* tongue, the perſonal pronouns are changed two or three ways,
according to the perſon they repreſent. E. G.
too and *u* ſignify *he* to or concerning a ſervant,
or perſon of low rank; *umba* and *undoeoe* expreſs
the ſame with tenderneſs and reſpect, as when a
father ſpeaks of his ſon; and inferiors apply the
words *tamunwahanſa, tu,* and *ohuwahanſa* to
their ſuperiors.

Alſo in the *Malayan* tongue a perſon addreſ-
ſing an equal ſays   *beta* I; to an inferior   *ako,* to a king   *patek,*

I shall illustrate the pronominal use of words under the other denominations by giving instances of each of them.

The *Demonstrative* pronouns (so called because they clearly *point out* and shew what we refer to). *Cato and Cicero were cotemporaries:* This *was famous for his eloquence, the* other *for his integrity.* In this sentence, the pronoun *this* is a substitute for the name of *Cicero,* in the circumstance of being named last; and *other* of *Cato,* as being only person who remained to be spoken of.

Possessive. His house, that is the house of some particular person mentioned before. These pronouns possessive have the same
use

---

or   *hamba,* which signifies a servant. In the same manner are *thou* and *he* expressed variously. *Reland. De linguis orientalibus.*

ufe as the Genitive cafes of their correfpond-
ent perfonal pronouns, being the fubftitutes of perfons under the character of poffef-
fors, or owners of the thing whofe name
they are joined with. *(a)*

Relative, referring to a noun or fentence
going before; as *The houfe which I have
built,* that is *which houfe.* The ufe of
this pronoun will be confidered more large-
ly in the conftruction of fentences. *(b)*

All

(a) The inhabitants of the *Caribbee* iflands
have a remarkable concife method of expreffing
the perfonal prononns; viz. by prefixing a fingle
letter to the word. *m* is my, *b* is thy, and *l* his;
as *nari,* my tooth; *bari,* thy tooth; and *lari,*
his tooth. *Reland de linguis Americanis.*

(b) The *French* language is peculiarly happy
in what their Grammarians call the *pronoun fupplying;* viz. *le, en, y;* being of vaftly more eafy
and extenfive application than any relative in o-
ther languages, as *Ils font heureux, et nous ne le
fommes pas.* They are happy, and we are not;

All thefe three kinds of Pronouns, as they refer to fome fubftantives with which (in languages that change the terminations of nouns on the account of number, cafe, &c.) they agree, and without which they have no determinate meanings, are of the nature of Adjectives.

In *Hebrew* not only Pronouns of the third perfon (as in all other languages) but

even

---

i. e. not happy; which is particularly referred to by the French *le*. *Newton vous plait, vous en parlez toujours*, You like *Newton*, you always fpeak of him. *Quand un homme eft mort, on n'y penfe plus;* when a man is dead, he is no more thought of.

The *French* pronoun *on* is likewife of as extenfive ufe as a nominative cafe to verbs, as the pronoun fupplying, which is governed of them; and in particular with the active voice of verbs is very elegantly made ufe of inftead of the paffive; as *on tint hier un confeil a Whitehall:* yefterday a counfil was held at Whitehall.

even the fecond perfon hath a diftinction of
fex,   being *thou man*, and
thou woman. (a)

The number of Pronouns is peculiarly
difficult to determine in all languages;
owing, not only to their being, in fact,
chiefly, adjectives; but alfo, to this, that
the fame term hath fometimes what is called
a pronominal ufe, and fometimes not; which
Grammarians have not fufficiently attended
to.

LECTURE

(a) The reafon why the third perfon admits
of the diftinction of gender more generally than
the firft and fecond, is becaufe the fex of the perfon fpoken of, who is abfent, cannot be known
without fome fuch provifion ; whereas it is unneceffary with refpect to the firft and fecond perfons, who are always prefent when they are mentioned.

LECTURE the SEVENTH.

OF

VERBS.

VERBS have been defined to be either the simple affirmation, which makes only one verb substantive, *(a)* or (as the actual structure of all languages obliges us to consider it) the union of the simple affirmation with another term expressing the state or condition of the subject concerning which

---

(a) It may perhaps be convenient to resolve even the verb substantive itself into a simple affirmation and an adjective or participle; since

which the affirmation is made. *(a)* A verb
therefore, being a complex word, admits
of as many modifications as each of the
ideas which it includes; and moreover
thofe which arife from the combination of
their feparate modifications.

The

---

fum, I am, may be confidered as containing the
three ideas expreffed by, *ego fum exiftens*, I am
being ; but the verb *fum*, in this laft fentence,
can admit of no farther refolution.

(a) Mr. *Harris*, after defining all verbs,
which are ftrictly fo called, to be words which
denote energies, is afterwards obliged to acknowledge that there are fome which appear to
denote nothing more than a mere fimple adjective, joined to an affertion; as , it
equalleth ; *albeo*, I am white, &c. But fince
thefe words, and many other of the fame nature,
are by all grammarians (whether juftly or not)
univerfally called verbs, and have the inflections
of verbs; is it not better to comprize them under the general definition of verbs? efpecially
fince they are all, with equal eafe, refolvable
into a fimple affirmation, joined to an adjective
or participle; which may be called an adjective
or attribute of time.

The ſtate or condition united with the ſimple affirmation is moſt commonly one which implies ſome energy, or the producing ſome effect, as *loving, eating, killing*. This effect may be produced by the ſubject of the affirmation, or it may take place upon it. This hath, in ſome languages, given occaſion to a two-fold diſtinction of verbs: for, in the former caſe, the verb is ſaid to be *active;* in the latter, it is differently terminated, and called *paſſive*. Thus when I ſay *Petrus amat, Peter loves,* the action of loving proceeds from Peter, and the verb is active, when I ſay *Petrus amatur, Peter is loved*. I mean that the action of loving terminates in, or takes place upon Peter, and the verb aſſumes a paſſive form.

In thoſe languages which admit of the diſtinction of verbs into active and paſſive, thoſe verbs which imply no idea of producing

ducing any effect out of the agent are called *Neuters*. As *Petrus fedet, Peter is fitting;* in which the ftate or condition that Peter is affirmed to be in doth not contain the idea of any effect which can pafs from one thing to another.

The *Hebrew*, *Greek*, and *Latin* languages contain this modification of verbs, but it is univerfally wanting in the modern *European* tongues, which exprefs the fame idea by feparating the affirmation from the word which expreffeth the ftate or condition of the fubject, when the meaning is intended to be paffive; and making ufe of fuch a term as conveys no other idea than that of receiving the effect; confining the ufual form of the verb to the active fenfe. In the fentence *Peter is killed*, the ftate killed, which is affirmed of Peter, implies receiving the effect, and the only fenfe that remains.

I for

for the fimple form of the verb, *(Peter kills)* is that of giving it.

A thing may not only be exprefsly affirmed, but may alfo be fpoken of under feveral reftrictions or limitations, and in connection with, or dependance upon other affirmations. Several of thefe manners or modes of fpeaking of an event have been felected, and made the foundation of a further diftinction of Moods or *Modes* in verbs. Of thefe the *Greeks* have the greateft number. The *English* admit none of them, but have recourfe to other methods of expreffing thofe circumftances of an affirmation, without giving a different modification to the verb. *(a)*

A direct unconditional affertion is in the *Indicative* mood.

(a) Except in one inftance; for I *am*, if I *be* are different modifications to exprefs different moods.

An event may be fpoken of as the will or command of another, as *fcribe, write thou.* This implies that it is the will or command of the perfon who fpeaks to the perfon fpoken to that he write: this is the *Imperative* mood. *(a)*

If one event do in any manner depend upon another event, the verb which expreffeth that which is not the principal, but only that which is the fecondary, and dependent event, is put in a mood called the *Subjunctive,* as *permitto ut fcribat,* I permit that he write. This mood is generally preceded by fome particle expreffing the connection or dependance of the fubjunctive fentence.

I 2   Sometimes

I 2

(a) In feveral languages, the fenfe of the imperative is often expreffed by the future and particularly with a negative, as *ne occideris,* thou fhalt not *kill.* In *Arabic* the imperative is never ufed but when the fenfe is affirmative.

Sometimes both the indicative fentence and the connecting participle are underftood, as *vivat rex*, let the king live: a verb denoting a wifh being underftood as, *opto ut rex vivat*, I wifh that the king may live: *veniat*, *he may come:* that is, *poteft fieri ut veniat.* In this cafe, when an event is fpoken of as only poffible, or liable to contingencies, the mood changes its name, but not its modification, and is called by the Latins the *Potential* mood.

An event mentioned as the wifh of any perfon conftitutes in *Greek* only, the *Optative* mood as   I wifh he may write.

It is eafy to fee that, upon thefe principles, moods might have been increafed almoft *ad infinitum:* fince the ways a fentence may be modified, or vary from a direct affertion,

fertion, are innumerable: for inftance, for the fame reafon that a *wifh* conftitutes a mood, an *interrogation* might conftitute one, a *permiffion* another, and fo on without end.

Laftly, the ftate or condition implied by the verb may not be affirmed of any other fubject, but be itfelf the fubject of an affirmation: in this cafe, it is faid to be in the *Infinitive* mood, as *videre eft jucundum, to fee is pleafant. videre*, here, is properly no verb, but the name of a power, act, ftate, or condition, and therefore a noun fubftantive. *(a)*

In *Latin*, inftead of ufing the infinitive mood

I 3

(a) The *Saxons* have an infinitive of a particular inflection, which they ufe as the *Latins* do their gerunds; as from an *to read* they fay

it is time of reading, or to read.

mood as a noun, in any other cafe than the *Nominative*, (as in the *Genitive*, *Accufative*, and *Ablative*) they give the word another form, and call it a *Gerund*, as *cupidus fcribendi*, *defirous of writing*; *peritus in fcribendo*, *fkilful in writing*; *promptus ad fcribendum*, *ready to write*: Whereas the *Greeks* were content to make ufe of the infinitive itfelf for that purpofe as

If the verb to which the gerund belongs be not neuter, the effect it expreffes may terminate fomewhere, and therefore gerunds require the fame cafes after them as the verbs themfelves: as *cupidus fcribendi libros*, *defirous of writing books*.

Still leaving out the affirmation, the action or ftate is fometimes expreffed by another noun, in one cafe only, varying in its ftructure from the former, and is called the *Supine*

Supine in um, as *eo piscatum*, *I go a fishing*, or *to fish*; which might have been expressed by the gerund, as *eo ad piscandum*. The *supine in u*, or the *latter supine*, is the same thing in the passive signification, that the former supine is in the active, as *difficile lectu*, *hard to be read*.

Lastly, the state or condition expressed by the verb without the affirmation is considered, in different circumstances, as a property be-longing to a person or thing, and is there-fore in all respects an adjective, though, (par-taking of the sense and time of the verb, and being derived from it) it be called a *Partici-ple*. Thus *amans loving*, implies the state or condition of one giving the effect; *amatus*, *loved*, the having received it; *amaturus*, *about to love*; the state of being about to give it; and *amandus*, *to be loved*, a state

of

of being to receive it. *(a)*

The fame idea derived ftom the verb may, in different circumftances, take the form of other adjectives, and even of fubftantives; as *amator, a lover,* or the perfon in whom love exifts as a power or paffion. But participles, having always been confidered as more particularly connected with verbs, it may fuffice in this place to have diftinctly pointed out their connection.

Some verbs, in the *Greek* and *Latin* languages, admit of modifications fimilar to the degrees of comparifon in adjectives: for, whereas the fimple verb directly affirms a certain ftate concerning the fubject of it, his

(a) In *Arabic* the participle is often expreffed by the future tenfe, following the preterite without a copula; as
venerunt flebunt, for *they came weeping.*

this modification, or rather, *derivative verb*
denotes only a tendency to it; thus *caleo*
signifies *to be hot, calefco, to begin to be hot.*
Thefe are called *Inceptives.* Another modification, or mode of derivation, intimates
a defire of the ftate, as *nupturio, I defire to
marry; bellaturio, I defire to be at war.*
Thefe are termed *Defideratives.*

An affirmation may be confidered with
refpect to the perfon that makes it, the perfon it is made to, and the perfon or thing
that is the fubject of it. Thefe being the
three perfons mentioned in the account of
pronouns, the change of terminations occafioned by thefe circumftances of an affirmation are called the *Perfons* of verbs. Thus
the Latins faid, *fcribo, I write; fcribis,
thou writeft;* and *fcribit, he writeth.*
They ufe likewife different terminations to
exprefs the plural perfons; as *fcribimus, we
write;*

write ; fcribitis, ye write ; fcribunt, they write. In *Englifh*, though we have invented different terminations to exprefs fome of the perfons, yet they are fo very few, that, to prevent ambiguity, we always ufe the perfonal pronouns along with the verbs, which there is no occafion for in *Latin, Greek* or *Hebrew.* Even the *French*, who diftinguifh all the perfons, do, neverthelefs, ufe them in conjunction with their correfponding pronouns, as *J'ame, Tu ames,* &c. *(a)*

LECTURE

(a) In the *Algonkine* tongue, fpoken by feveral nations of *North-America*, the perfons of verbs are denoted, in moft inftances, by a fingle letter or fyllable prefixed to the verb ; as *nifakia,* I love ; *kifakia, thou loveft ; oufakia, he loveth,* &c. *Reland de linguis Americanis.*

LECTURE the EIGHTH.

OF

VERBS.

HAD mankind nothing to exprefs but their prefent apprehenfions, as *the air is hot;* or univerfal truths, that have no relation to time, as *God is eternal ;* the fimple affirmation would be fufficient; but in order to fpeak of things paft and future, as well as prefent, it was found convenient to introduce a further modification into verbs, to make them capable of exprefling thefe different circumftances of time.

This

This is the foundation of the different
TENSES of verbs: and as time *paſt* and
future may be divided into time more or leſs
paſt, and time to come at a greater or leſſer
diſtance; alſo into paſt and future with reſpect to other events connected with them,
many languages admit of a great number of
tenſes: but in no language have they been
formed upon any accurately juſt and commodious diviſion of time.   I ſhall mention
ſome of the principal diſtinctions of time
that have been actually obſerved in languages.

Time *preſent* is invariable: in no language, therefore, is there more than one
Preſent tenſe. (a)

An

(a) Some Grammarians, conſidering every
action, whether paſt preſent or to come, as
either *doing*, or *done*, ſay that there is properly a

An event may be paſt when it is ſpoken
of, but have been preſent when another
K   event,

perfect and imperfect in all the three tenſes; but
though time paſt and future, being of indefinite
extent, may admit of any ſubdiviſion; time preſent, being properly nothing more than a point,
cannot be analogous to them in that reſpect.
It ſeems, therefore, to be more natural to refer
every action which is compleated at the time of
ſpeaking of it to the preterite tenſes, and not to
the preſent: and, therefore, that *ſcripſi*, I have
written, referring to an action that is confeſſed-
ly paſt, is a preterite tenſe; and not (as the accurate *Dr. Clarke* and others who have followed
him would term it) a perfect preſent.

The *Hebrew* and *Arabick* tongues have no
method of expreſſing time preſent but by the
participle, as   I watching,
for I watch.   The *Welch* language alſo hath no
preſent tenſe, except the verb ſubſtantive and
two other irregular verbs: inſtead of it, they
uſe a circumlocution of the infinitive mood, as
yr wyf yn caru, which, rendered literally, is *I
am into love*, i. e. I am loving, for I love.   In
the *Poconchi* tongue, ſpoken in ſome parts of
Honduras, the circumſtances of a diſcourſe doth
generally diſtinguiſh the preſent from the future.
Gage's ſurvey of the Weſt Indies.

event, which is either mentioned or referred to, took place; as *when Peter entered I was writing, ſcribebam.* The writing was paſt when it was ſpoken of, but preſent when Peter entered. This is called the *Imperfect tenſe:* or it may be ſpoken of as paſt in general, without giving any intimation when it was preſent, as *ſcripſi epiſtolam, I have written a letter,* which may have been in any period of time paſt extending to the preſent. This is called the *Preterperfect tenſe;* or laſtly it may be mentioned not only as paſt at the time when it is ſpoken of, but as alſo paſt when another event, referred to in the ſentence, was paſt; as *when Peter entered I had writen a letter, ſcripſeram.* Which expreſſes, that the letter was written both when it was ſpoken of, and alſo when Peter entered

tered.   This is called the *Preterpluperfect tense.* (*a*)

We speak of a thing to come as future indefinitely with respect to the time of mentioning it, as *scribam, I shall write;* or, though future with respect to the time of speaking of it, yet as past with relation to some other event; as *when Peter shall enter I shall have written, scripsero.* The action is said to be future to the time of speaking of it, but as

K 2   past

(*a*) In *Welch* the infinitive mood is made to supply the place of the *preter-pluperfect tense* of the subjunctive mood, the preposition *wedi,* after, being placed before the nominative case; as *wedi ir gwr lefaru, after to the man speak;* or more exactly in Greek,

; instead of *after the man had spoken.*

paſt with reſpect to Peter's entering. *(a)*

The Greeks make more diſtinctions of time, both paſt and future, one of their *futures* is called the *Paulopoſtfuturum*, as being generally ſuppoſed to expreſs an event which is about to happen very ſoon: it hath a paſſive ſignification; as

juſt going to be beaten. *(b)*

I

(a) The *Welch* have no determinate future indicative: to ſupply it, they have recourſe to a periphraſis, in which the infinitive mood is introduced; as *mi a fyddaf yn ys griſennu:* which, rendered literally, is *I ſhall be in to write;* inſtead of *I ſhall write:* or as in *Greek,* we ſhould ſay
inſtead of   ,

(b) It is remarkable that in the *Hebrew* and *Arabic* tongues the two only tenſes they have, viz. the *preterite* and *future* are each convertible into the other; and ſometimes into the preſent, by prefixing certain particles; which, however, do not belong to the verb, but have a ſeparate

I am very far from afferting that the foregoing account of the diftinction of moods and tenfes will be found to correfpond with every ufe that is made of them; much lefs, that every perfon who hath written in any language hath conformed to it. As languages were not made by Philofophers, but fug-gefted by the neceffities of beings in their firft uncultivated ftate, and enlarg-

ed

fignification. In the *Hebrew*   which fig-nifies *and*, prefixed to the preter, makes it have the fenfe of the future; fometimes of the prefent : and the fame   , prefixed to the future, al-ways changes its fignification, generally into the preter, but fometimes into the prefent. E. G.
            is *I vifited*;   and *I will vifit*;   is *he will fay*;
            and be faid.
In *Arabic* the future hath the fenfe of the preterite when   *am not* ; or
ama   *not yet*   are prefixed to it : more-over, according to other particles prefixed, either of the tenfes may have the fenfe of the prefent, preterite, future, optative, or fubjunctive.

ed as their further occafions prompted and required; it is in vain to expect that the laws and rules of them fhould be either perfectly natural, or confiftent. All that was necef-fary in lectures upon *Univerfal Grammar* was to give fuch a defcription of any parti-cular mode of fpeech as will agree with the general practice of thofe who ufed it, with-out taking notice of thofe deviations which fall within the provin ce of particular Gram-marians.

It were to be wifhed, indeed, for the eafe of underftanding and ufing a language, particularly a dead one, that the principles of it were more uniform; but this is an ad-vantage which no language can boaft. Nei-ther the *Greeks*, nor *Latins* have, in all refpects, preferved a perfect diftinction among their moods and tenfes: for, define thefe terms as we will, and lay down what rules

rules we please with respect to them, we
shall find exceptions to them in the best and
purest classics.

Only the most perfect intelligence, who
can see the whole at one view, can establish
laws that have no exceptions. The works
of nature, indeed, we have reason to believe, are throughout uniform; and in
analyzing the works of nature, in which so
much uniformity hath been actually observed, it may be useful to have a view to the
most simple and uniform laws; as those,
from past experience, will have strong pre-
sumptions in their favour: but this clue
will by no means serve our purpose in ex-
plaining what hath been the invention of
men, and particularly of rude uncultivated
men. We must consider their circumstances,
make the best we can of a lame and imperfect subject, and not deny real defects
and

and redundancies, or fruitlefsly labour to reconcile manifeft inconfiftencies, but muft ourfelves conform to eftablifhed vicious practices, if we would not make ourfelves juftly ridiculous by our fingularity.

The CONJUGATIONS of verbs like the declenfions of nouns are not modifications that are founded on the nature of things, but merely on the cafual form of the words in particular languages; according to which the principal tenfes in all moods conform to a particular analogy. Thus *amo* *I love*, in Latin, is faid to be of the *firft conjugation;* having its radical tenfes, *amo, amavi, amatum, amare;* and *moneo*, *I advife*, of the *fecond;* having its radical tenfes, *moneo monui, monitum, monere.* The formation of thefe radical tenfes are very irregular: but the rules for the formation of other tenfes from thefe admit of very few exceptions.

Thus

Thus the *Plufquamperfectum* is formed univerfally from the *perfect* by changing (i)
into (eram) as amavi, amaveram. *(a)*

In

(a) In *Arabick* Grammars we find thirteen
conjugations, nine of thofe which have three
radicals in the third perfon preterite (which is
always the root from which all inflexions are fuppofed to be made in all the *Eaftern* tongues of
that genus, or family as we may call it) and four
of thofe which have four radicals: and in
Hebrew there are feven conjugations. But what
the Grammarians of the *Arabick* and *Hebrew*
tongues call *conjugations*, are not fo properly conjugations, in the fenfe in which other Grammarians ufe that term, as *moods*; becaufe the fame
verb may admit of all the conjugations: but as
each of thefe is further modified into the indicative, imperative, and infinitive moods, the
Grammarians, not chufing to call thefe *moods of
moods*, thought proper to call the one conjugations, and the other moods. Befides, both in
Hebrew and *Arabick*, what, in other languages, is
called the *paffive voice* is found among the conjugations. Strictly fpeaking, Grammarians of
thefe languages make but one conjugation of
them, and all verbs, that do not conform to the
common manner of inflection are promifcuoufly

In *Hebrew*, and other eaftern languages, verbs are inflected according to *gender* as well as nouns: thus   is *thou man didft vifit*, and   is *thou wo-man diaft vifit*.   They alfo admit of com-parifon, or at leaft what may be called ex-aggeration; as   *He broke*, *he broke to pieces*.   They have likewife a particular modification of the verb, to ex-prefs one perfon's caufing another to do a thing; as from   *he reigned he made to reign,* and another when the action of the verb is reciprocal, or reverts upon the fubject of it, as from   *he was holy   he made himfelf holy*, or *he pretended to be holy*.

Very

called *irregulars;* whereas the feveral kinds of thefe might have been called conjugations.

The *Arabians,* among other conjugations, have one to exprefs *co-operation*, expreffed in *Latin* by the prepofition *con* prefixed to the verb: another fignifies *petition* and *confeffion*.

Very few of these modifications of verbs are used in modern *European* languages, and particularly in *English*, but we supply this defect of modifications by auxiliary verbs; as *to be*, *to have*, *will*, *shall*, *can*, *must*, &c. as *I will write*, for *scribam. (a)* It is apparent, from this example, that the affirmation, with all the circumstances attending it, is transferred from what is usually called the *principal verb* to the auxiliary, leaving the word which, in other languages, implies both the affirmation and circumstances, nothing more than the indefinite idea of the action, condition, or state which is affirmed

(a) Neverthelefs, in all the dialects of the *Teutonic*, the participle of the preterite is formed by prefixing an augment (ge) like that of the *Greeks* before the word ; as in the prefent *German*, *Ich hab gehabt*, I have had. In the *Saxon* tongue this was afterwards changed into *y*, which was common even in *English* in *Chaucer's* time; as *ycleapt.*

affirmed of the fubject: in fhort a mere participle: in modern languages they, accordingly, remain unchanged, and all the modifications peculiar to the verb take place in the auxiliary. *(a)*

Which is abfolutely the moft commodious expreffion

(a) But the *Malayan* tongue, which is of great extent, and in great efteem in the *Eaft-Indies*, far exceeds our northern *European* tongues in fimplicity: for, in that language, the verb itfelf admits of no modification whatever, on account either of perfon, tenfe, or voice: in all thefe refpects the perfonal pronouns only, with particles prefixed, determine the fenfe. E. G. *poekol* fignifies *to beat*. In the perfect tenfe they fay *beta foedda poekol*, I have beaten. In the future *beta adda poekol*, I fhall beat. In the paffive voice *fjadi poekol* is to be beaten.

The *Brafilian* tongue hath only two modifications of verbs, of which one is *pofitive*, and the other *negative*; as *aincu*, I kill; *namcai*, I do not kill. *Reland ubi fu, ra.*

expreſſion of affirmations and their circumſtances is not very eaſy to determine. I
think, however, it may be ſaid, in favour
of the modern method, that we can expreſs
all the ideas included in, or connected with
an affirmation, with more preciſion, and
almoſt as few additional ſyllables as the
Greeks or *Latins*. And ſome very important circumſtances of an affirmation are
expreſſed in *Engliſh*, particularly, with the
utmoſt conciſeneſs and preciſion, for which
in thoſe languages we muſt have recourſe to
very long praiphraſes. For a proof of this
let any perſon endeavour to expreſs in *Latin*
the difference between, *I ſhall* and *I will
write; I may*, and *I can write.*

The diſtinction that ſome Grammarians
make of verbs into *perſonal* and *imperſonal*
hath ro foundation in reaſon; for every affirmation muſt neceſſarily imply ſome ſub-

L   ject

ject of which it is affirmed: Thus *pluit,*
which we render *it rains,* supplying the
elipsis is *cælum* or *aer pluit.*

LECTURE

LECTURE the NINTH.

OF

ADVERBS, &c.

IRREGULARITIES

AND

DIALECTS.

OF ADVERBS it hath been obferved, that they are chiefly *contractions for other words*, and fometimes for whole fen-tences. *(a)*   This is very evident with re-

fpect

(a) Mr. *Harris* calls *Adverbs*, *Attributives of Attributives;* that is of *verbs*, or *adjectives;* as if they always attended thofe parts of fpeech, and modified their fignification.   But they are only

fpeƈt to the three principal Claſſes of them,
namely thoſe of *time, place* and *quality* or
manner: for inſtance, *nunc* may be rendered by *hoc tempore; hic,* by *hoc loco;* and
ſic, by *hoc modo.* The affirmation *yes* ſerves
inſtead of repeating a whole ſentence, with
its ſubjeƈt, affirmation, and every thing belonging to it: *non, not* is the ſame as *nego,*

or

thoſe of *quality* or *manner* which can, without
great force, be comprehended in the definition;
and many words muſt be excluded which have
ſo long, and ſo univerſally been called *adverbs,*
that it is making too free with words and their
eſtabliſhed acceptation not to include them in it.
For inſtance, by what conſtruƈtion can, *ſurſum
hucuſque, ſemel, cur,* and many others be called
the attributes of verbs. If nothing more be
meant by the definition, than that adverbs are
words which ſerve to aſcertain and fix an affirmation, every word in the ſentence is an adverb;
at leaſt all the words into which adverbs may be
reſolved, which are both ſubſtantives, adjeƈtives,
and even verbs themſelves.

or serves instead of repeating the subject and affirmation of a sentence with contrary attributes. *(a)*

Adverbs of quality or manner admit of comparison for the same reason that their correspondent adjectives do : for as *sapiens*, *wise*, may be varied into *sapientior*, *wiser*, *sapientissimus*, *wisest*; so may *sapienter*, *wisely*

L 3

(a) Notwithstanding a preposition be sufficiently known to be affirmative by the absence of the negative particles, the *Welch* language hath a particle [a] appropriated to signify an affirmation; as, *mi a garaf*, *I love*.

In several languages a double negative often only serves to encrease the force of a single one as in Greek
let no one
it is not possible. In *Saxon*, *ne om ic na Chriſt*, I am not the Chriſt. In *French Je ne parle pas*, I do not speak. In *Engliſh* and *Latin* the second negative deſtroys the firſt, and makes the sentence affirmative; as *non poſſum non meminiſſe*, I cannot forget.

wifely, become *fapientius, more wifely*, and *fapientiffime, moft wifely*. Though it is not every language which admits of the comparifon of adjectives that alfo admits of the comparifon of adverbs.

Adverbs, being contractions for other words, fuch words have, in fome languages, been made adverbs as had much better have been left in the clafs to which their fignification gave them a claim; as *utinam, I wifh*, which is a verb: likewife *eja, age, agedum, come on; heu, eheu, ehodum, come hither:* and *en, eccus, eccum, behold him,* and feveral others.

PREPOSITIONS are words which, in all languages, have been invented to exprefs the relation or fituation of one word to another; for the cafes of nouns can exprefs but a few of thofe relations. Almoft all prepofitions,

in

in their original acceptation, relate to *local position*; as *with, at, from, without* &c. the best method, therefore, of ascertaining their proper use in construction, and when applied by analogy, to things that are not sensible, but intellectual, moral, &c. is to attend to the figure, and consider what preposition would best express the relation, as of sensible things to sensible things: thus a paraphrase *on* the scriptures is proper, because in the latent figure, the one is conceived to lie or rest as it were upon the other.

Prepositions admit of no inflections in any language, unless some of them may be said to be compared; though, in that case, they are considered as *adjectives:* as *near him, nearer him;* because it may be said that in this case another preposition to is understood;

as *near to him, nearer to him. (a)*

Of Conjunctions more will be faid
when I treat of the *conftruction of fentences*,
I only obferve, in this place, that they may
be claffed into as many divifions and fub-
divifions as there are different manners in
which we can pafs from one fentence to
another, which are as numerous as the relations which one fentence may ftand in to
another. Thus fome are termed *copulative*,
as *and;* and fome *disjunctive*, as *or; illa-
tive*, as *therefore; exceptive*, as *unlefs*, &c.
the meaning of which the names themfelves
(which

(a) *Prepofitions*, in moft languages, precede
their fubftantives; but fometimes they follow
them, and are even affixed to them in Latin; as
genuum tenus; up to the knees; *mecum*, with me.
In the *Brafilian* tongue prepofitions always take
the form of affixes; as *cou*, upon; *itacou*, upon
a ftone. *Reland de linguis Americanis.*

(which may be found in almoſt every grammar of every language) ſufficiently expreſs. *(a.)*

Except the ſimple conjunctives, and diſjunctives *and, or., either,* &c. and *as* and *than* which are terms of compariſon; all the other conjunctions, as they ſhew the dependance that one ſentence hath upon another, expreſs ſome modification of the relation of cauſe and effect; as will appear by conſidering any of them ſeparately: let the trial be made with the principal of them, ſuch as *if, but although, becauſe, therefore, that,* &c.

INTER-

(a) I ſay that conjunctions connect ſentences: for though they be ſometimes placed between two ſingle words, they ſerve to contract and unite different ſentences; as *Brutus and Caſſius fought* may be reſolved into *Brutus fought,* and *Caſſius fought.*

INTERJECTIONS paſs into words of the other claſſes, by the ſame gradations by which inarticulate ſounds paſs into articulate. Thus though ſome words be evidently inarticulate expreſſions of ſudden paſſions and emotions, as *ha ha he*, in laughing, and convey no particular idea; others, which have, notwithſtanding, been called interjections, are in part articulate, and others are wholly ſo: as *væ* an expreſſion of ſorrow; *papæ* of admiration; *euge* of encouragement: ſome of which, as they may be rendered by either words, ought rather to be called *Adverbs*.

Beſides the words reduced to the abovementioned claſſes, which have each a diſtinct meaning, or joint value in a diſcourſe, Grammarians enumerate others, which they call *Expletives*, as adding nothing to the ſenſe where they are introduced, but ſerving only

only to improve the found; as   and
others in *Greek*. They feem, however,
to add fomething to the emphafis, though it
be fmall. It is very common for words,
and particularly verbs, in *Latin*, *Greek*,
and *Hebrew;* to receive a fuperfluous termination for the fake of found: for inftance
mutarier, for *mutair:* alfo a [t] inferted
between two *French* words is of no other ufe
than to prevent the concurrence of two
vowels; as *a-t-il, hath he*. For a like
reafon, it is ufual with writers in all languages to fhorten words upon occafion, both
at the beginning, the middle, and the end;
but to make much ufe of thefe orthographi-
cal figures, or licences, in any language,
is not admired.

The inflexions of words are not precifely
the fame in words of the fame claffes; but,
in all languages, are fubject to very confiderable

derable *irregularities*. Thefe irregularities chiefly affect words of the moft frequent occurrence, which are alfo generally fhort, and foon pronounced; as *fum*, *I am*; *fui*, *I have been*. Moreover, inftead of a fimple inflexion, it frequently happens that quite other words are introduced, to exprefs the different modifications; as *bonus good*; *melior better*; *optimus beft*, &c.

Thefe facts, if attended to, will lead us to the fource of thefe irregularities. Words of neceffary and frequent occurrence muft have been peculiarly liable to be pronounced with great variation, by different perfons, and in different parts of a country. It would alfo frequently happen that perfons would hit upon quite different words to exprefs the fame idea. And when, in confequence of a perfect communication between all the parts of a country, thofe forms

forms of fpeech would grow eftablifhed which had the moft, and the moft powerful advocates; in this cafe, it could not but happen fometimes, that the inflections of different words of the fame meaning would be intermixed, and produce what we now call an irregular inflection.   To give an in-ftance of this: the verb *fum* was ufed for the verb fubftantive in fome parts of *Italy*, and the verb *fuo* in others: when all that fpoke the language had a perfect communication, and it became neceffary to adopt one form, it happened that the verb *fum* was retained in the prefent tenfe; but *fui* (from *fuo*) in the perfect; and *fuo* in the prefent became obfolete. *(a)*

M   This

(a) Thus in *Greek*   he bought,
but never   I bought, inftead of
which they ufed

This might alfo be a fource of many de
fective words: fince, though they might
originally be ufed in all tenfes, moods, and
perfons; yet there being alfo other words,
of the fame fignification, in ufe in different
parts of a country; one verb might be preferred in one tenfe, mood, or perfon, and
another in another. *(a)* For the fame
reafon, many *nouns* alfo are now of different genders, in different numbers, and even
in the fame number; and have fome cafes
formed according to one declenfion, and
others according to another, and fometimes
according to feveral; with every other fpecies of *Heteroclify* that can be imagined.
Genders

(a) Meurfius in his Comments on *Helladius*
an ancient Grammarian, gives many inftances
in which the *Greeks* made ufe of fome certain
tenfes of verbs without ever ufing the other tenfes and often the third perfon without the others.

Genders and inflections being perfectly arbitrary, there could not be any univerfally fatisfactory reafon why one mere cuftom fhould not take place as well as another, which had no better foundation in nature.

When a language was fpoken by feveral independant cities or ftates, that had no very free communication with one another, and before the ufe of letters was fo generally diffufed as to fix the modes of it, it was impoffible, not only to prevent the fame words being pronounced with different tones of voice (like the *Englifh* and *Scotch* pronunciation) but even the number and nature of the fyllables would be greatly altered when the original root remained the fame; and even quite different words would be introduced in different places. And when, upon the introduction of letters, men endeavoured to exprefs their founds in writing, they

M 2   would,

would, of courfe, write their words with
the fame varieties in letters.   Thefe different modes of fpeaking and writing a language originally the fame have obtained the
name of DIALECTS, and are moſt of all
confpicuous in the *Greek* tongue, thus
I was, by the *Attics*, frequently pronounced   ; by the *Dorians*
and   ; and by the *Boetians*
and

All thefe different modes of fpeaking,
like all other modes, might have grown into
difrepute, and, by degrees out of ufe, giving place to one as a ſtandard, had particular
circumſtances contributed to recommend
and enforce it ; but, in *Greece*, every fe-
perate community looking upon itfelf as in
no refpect inferior to its neighbours in point
of antiquity, dignity, intelligence, or any
other qualification; and being conſtantly ri-
vals

vals for power, wealth, and influence, would no more fubmit to receive the laws of language from another than the laws of government: rather, upon the introduction of letters and learning, they would vye with each other in embellifhing and recommending their own dialeâs, and thereby perpetuate thofe different modes of fpeech.

On the other hand, in a country where all that fpoke the language had one head, all writers, ambitious to draw the attention of the leading men in the ftate, would ftudioufly throw afide the particular forms of fpeaking they might happen to have been brought up in, and conform to that of their fuperiors: by this means Dialeâs, though ufed in converfation, would hardly ever be introduced into writing; and the written language would be capable of being reduced very nearly to a perfeâ uniformity.

M 3

For

For this reaſon the language of *Greece*, though ſpoken at firſt within a very ſmall extent of country, yet by a number of independent cities, had no common ſtandard; and books now extant in it differ ſo widely in their forms of expreſſion; that the moſt accurate ſkill in ſome of them will not enable a man thoroughly to underſtand others. Let any perſon after reading *Homer* or *Heſiod* take up *Theocritus*. Whereas, in the *Latin* tongue, though written in very diſtant parts of the vaſt *Roman* empire, Dialects are unknown. However differently *Romans* might ſpeak, there are no more differences in their writings than the different genius, abilities, and views of different men will always occaſion. The *Patavinity* of Livy is not to be perceived.

When a language had been ſpoken by different nations a conſiderable time before
the

the introduction of letters and learning, the variations in the forms of fpeech would grow too confiderable to form only different dialects of the fame language; when reduced to writing they would form what are called *fifter-languages*, analogous in their ftructure, and having many words in common. Thus the *Hebrew* and *Chaldaic* or *Syriac* with perhaps other eaftern languages, might have been originally the fame. On the other hand, the *Englifh* and *Scotch*, had the kingdoms continued feparate, might have been diftinct languages, having two different ftandards of writing.

LECTURE

LECTURE the TENTH.

OF

DERIVATION

AND

SYNTAX.

IN a manner analogous to the various inflections of words of the same class, whereby the idea that any of them represent is differently circumstanced, and yet the word remains a *substantive, adjective, verb,* &c. as before, are the ideas themselves, as

it

it were, inflected; fo as to take the form of different parts of fpeech, and yet retain the fame meaning and original fignification in them all. Rather it may be called the *Tranfmutation* of words: for, as in the feigned tranfmutation of metals, the matter, the fubftance, of the metal is fuppofed to remain the fame, though the external fenfible properties, whereby it was denominated this or that particular metal, be changed: In like manner, though, in this cafe, an idea appear now in the form of a fubftantive, then of an adjective, again a verb, or an adverb, it is in reality the fame idea ftill: only differently modified, and having different external properties. To inftance in the word *homo,* a *man:* the fame idea conftitutes the adjective *humanus, belonging to a man;* and the adverb *humaniter, like a man.*

Participles,

Participles, and particular prepofitions, alfo, prefixed or affixed to words, do greatly diverfify the meaning of them, and, in a very eafy, and commodious manner, enlarge and enrich a language; as from *humanus, humane* comes *inhumanus, inhuman;* and from the Englifh word *hope* comes *hopeful*, and *hopelefs*. As thefe feveral prefixes and affixes have a fixed and determinate meaning, at the fame time that the ufe of them greatly enlargeth a language, it adds nothing to the difficulty of learning and ufing it; for the meaning of the compound word is eafily deduced from the known parts of which it confifts.

Moreover, not only are words that have a meaning joined to particles that have no meaning in themfelves, but alfo to other words that have a diftinct and feparate fignification; as   , *vainglorious;*

ous; which words, in their respective languages, are formed by the union of two other words, which have separately a distinct signification, and which they retain in conjunction.

From these various compositions of words is derived the chief copia and power of the *Greek* language: for the *Greek primitives* do not exceed those of other languages in number, and hence the comparative poverty of the *Hebrew* and some other *Eastern tongues* of a like simple structure. It is observable of those languages that do not easily admit of such compositions of words, that if they do, notwithstanding, in a course of time, acquire a large stock, it is at the expence of making them infinitely difficult to the learner. The *Arabic*, with no more words than the *Greek*, is said to have prodigiously more roots, and the difficulty of

learning

learning a language depends chiefly upon the number of its original roots : for when they are once learned, and the method of combining them become familiar, the combinations themfelves give the learner but little trouble; as when a perfon is perfect in the alphabet of a language he foon learns to read it.

This combination of words and the ufes of it may be likewife illuftrated by the doctrine of fimple and compound ideas in the human mind. Our fimple ideas are few, and the chief furniture of an improved mind muft confift of compound ideas, formed by the various combinations of fimple ones. In like manner, the copia of a well formed language confifts of compound words, formed by the combinations of fimple roots.

Of

Of S Y N T A X.

HAVING, in the preceding lectures, considered the principal affections of single words, I come now to treat of sentences; which is the subject of that part of Grammar which is usually called SYNTAX.

A *sentence* is either single, or compound; and a period consists, either of one sentence, or a combination of sentences, joined by particles expressing the relation that each sentence hath to the succeeding.

A single sentence consists of a single affirmation, or a subject and attribute, joined by a verb; as *God is invisible.* In this sentence, *God* is the *subject* of the affirmation, and *invisible* is the *attribute,* or that

N   which

which is affirmed of the fubject, the verb *is* ferving to exprefs the affirmation.

In a compound fentence, the fubject or attribute, or both, are made complex terms, capable of being themfelves refolved into diftinct fingle fentences, or even into lefs compound fentences. This fentence *God who is invifible made the world which is vifible* is compound, both the fubject and attribute containing, each of them, diftinct affirmations; the former, that *God is invifible,* and the latter, that *the world is vifible.*

Here, likewife, is apparent the principal ufe of the relative *who* or *which;* namely, that the fentence to which it belongs doth not contain the principal affirmation, but one that is either introductory, or fubfequent to it: that is, the relative ferves as a common *link* or *vinculum* to join what may be called

called *incidental* affirmations to the principal one, in order to make a compound sentence. If I say *God is invisible*, the sense is complete, nothing further is expected; but if I say *God who is invisible*, though the words contain a real affirmation; yet it is so circumstanced, by means of the relative *who*, that the mind is in suspense, waiting for another, and the principal affirmation, or something to affirm concerning God, who is invisible.

There is no necessity, however, for expressing the introductory and subsequent affirmations directly; since the structure of most languages will admit of the relative being suppressed and implied. For the sentence is equally intelligible whether I say, *God who is invisible made the world which is visible;* or *the invisible God made the visible world.* The only difference is, that,

N 2

in

in the former cafe, the incidental affirmation is more particularly pointed out, to draw the attention the more, and hath the greater emphafis; whereas, in the latter, though the fame affertion be expreffed, it is in a more flight and fuperficial manner.

By the fame fteps, the fubject or attribute of a prepofition may be made ftill more complex at pleafure, and yet be but one compound fentence; as every relative and its verb, either expreffed or underftood, ftill points forward or backward to one principal affirmation. Thus the following is but one fentence. *The all-wife, almighty, and infinitely good, but invifible God made the vifible world, with all its furniture and inhabitants; confifting of land, and water, mountains, rivers, trees, men, birds, beafts, fifhes, and innumerable other things, which difplay his perfections.* For all the terms that are annexed

annexed to the fubject and predicate only make thofe two ideas the more complex, by a diftinct enumeration of their properties.

Or, though the additional words in a fen-tence exprefs a circumftance of the affirma-tion, and be not a defcription either of the fubject or attribute, the fentence is ftill but fingle; as *Solomon decided concerning the dead child very wifely:* in this place *wifely,* in whatever part of the fentence it be infert-ed, expreffes a circumftance of the affirma-tion; implying that Solomon not only decid-ed, but decided wifely, or with wifdom; the adverb, as obferved above, being a con-traction for that periphrafis.

In any other cafe, where diftinct affirma-tions are made, and the relative with its verb is neither expreffed nor underftood, **the** whole is not one compound fentence, but a combination of fentences; and if no paufe be made in the difcourfe between them, a conjunction, expreffing their relation to one another, is either expreffed or underftood; as *I will write, unlefs you prevent me:* Here are two affirmations, *I will write,* and *you will prevent me.* And, it being impoffible to infert the relative with its verb between them, they muft be confidered as diftinct fentences, the conjunction *unlefs* fhowing what relation they ftand in to one another: in this place, it implies, that the two affirmations are of fuch a nature, that if the latter take place, the former cannot.

Any number of thefe fentences, fimple or compound, make a *period;* and any number of periods, a *paragraph.* The relation which periods, and even paragraphs, have to one another is expreffed by the fame conjunctive particles which ferve to connect

the

the members of compound sentences; though, for the greater clearnefs and perfpicuity of compofition, it is preferable (efpecially in argumentation) after a complete paragraph, to fhow the relation of the next paragraph by a fentence appropriated to that purpofe. For inftance if, in the laft mentioned example, inftead of a thing which is fo foon expreffed as the writing of a letter, a number of things of confequence, which required a larger explication and detail of particulars, had been propofed; and, inftead of a fimple prohibition, other fchemes, which required to be mentioned diftinctly were in danger of interfering with the former, a judicious compofer would not, in this cafe, chufe to connect thefe two details with the fimple conjunctive particle *unlefs;* but in a much larger and more explicite manner: as *but before thefe fchemes can be put in execution, it muft be confidered*

*ed how far they may interfere with others,
of no less importance;* or some other introduction to the same purpose.

It is in these forms of transition from sentence to sentence, and paragraph to paragraph, or the connexion of the different
sentences and parts of a discourse, that the
chief difficulty of composition, in point of
elegance, consists. Some connect the materials of their compositions in a more obvious and direct, others in a more concealed
and indirect manner; some enlarge upon the
relations of the several parts, and thereby
make their discourse more diffuse; others in
a manner suppress the connecting particles,
and by that means are concise; and it requires judgment to determine when the one
method, and when the other is preferable.

But this can no more be taught by written

ten rules, except in a grofs general manner, than the art of graceful motion, or dancing, can be taught by written rules. Both are habits, which can only be acquired and perfected by obfervation, and repeated trials· A graceful motion may be perceived, and pointed out when it is feen; but to defcribe a *priori*, or before hand in what it muft confift, were impoffible. In like manner, the beft and moft graceful tranfitions muft be learned from the obfervation of the practice of the beft writers, and can be learned no way elfe.

LECTURE

LECTURE the ELEVENTH.

OF THE

CONCATENTION

OF

SENTENCES

AND

TRANSPOSITION

OF

WORDS.

THE concatention of sentences, may supply us with a pretty good teft of the fimplicity or refinement of languages. It is very late before children learn the ufe use of connecting particles in sentences; and persons must have seen read, and conversed, if not have written a good deal, before they be ready and accurate in the use of a considerable variety of them.

Now the method of learning and using a language that is formed must be analogous to the method of its formation at first. Short and unconnected sentences would be sufficient for the most pressing and necessary occasions of human life, of men acquainted but with a few objects, and only the most obvious qualities of those objects : As human life improved, as men became acquainted with a greater variety and multiplicity of objects, and new relations were perceived to subsist among them, they would find themselves under a necessity of inventing new terms to express them. As their growing experience and observation would furnish

them

them with a greater stock of ideas to communicate, and subjects to consult and converse about, their endeavours to express
their new conceptions of things would lead
them, by degrees, and after repeated trials,
into every requisite form of transition, for
the purpose of connected discourse, either
of the historical, or augmentative kind.

But, as we find that persons who have
not learned to read and write are in a great
measure incapable of a connected discourse,
and even persons who are accustomed to read
and converse with ease are seldom able, at
first, to put their thoughts together in writing with tolerable propriety ; it is not easy
to conceive, that the language of any people, before the introduction of letters, could
be otherwise than very incoherent and unconnected: and that their first attempts to
write would want that variety, accuracy and
elegance

elegance of contexture, which their late compofitions would acquire.

Hence the ftriking fimplicity of ftyle in the books of the *old teftament;* perhaps the moft ancient writings in the world. The hiftory of *Mofes* how different from that of *Livy*, and *Thucidides;* or even of *Cæfar*, *Salluft*, and *Zenophon*. The moral dif-courfes of *Solomon*, how different from thofe of *Plato*, *Cicero* and *Seneca*: for though much time had elapfed from *Mofes* to *Solomon;* yet the *Hebrew* nation, not having been addicted to letters in that inter-val, their language had received little or no improvement.

Even the writers of the *new teftament*, having been chiefly converfant with the an-cient *Jewifh* writers, and their education having given them no leifure to attend to

O   the

the refinements of ftyle, have generally a-
dopted the fimple unconnected ftyle of their
forefathers, both in their narration and
reafoning. I fhall give one inftance of this.
John the evangelift is giving an account of
a converfation that paffed between *John the
baptift*, and the *Jews*; inftead of carrying
on the narration in his own perfon, as an
hiftorian, and giving the queftions and anfwers fuch a form as was proper to make
them incorporate with his own account of
them (a turn quite familiar to other writers)
he reports the words juft as they were fpoken,
notwithftanding the fpeeches were too fhort
to make it in the leaft neceffary or expedient
to fet down the whole by way of formal
dialogue.

John I. 19. *And this is the record of
John, when the* JEWS *fent priefts and
Levites from* JERUSALEM *to afk him Who
art*

art thou? And he confeſſed, and denied not; but confeſſed, I am not the Chriſt. And they aſked him, What then art thou? Elias? and he ſaid I am not. Art thou the prophet? and he anſwered no.

This conversation a writer uſed to com-poſition would rather have related in a more connected manner, as follows. *Then the Jews ſent prieſts and Levites from Jeruſalem to aſk him who he was, and he confeſſed he was not the Chriſt: They aſked him if he was Elias, but he ſaid he was not, if he was that prophet, but he anſwered no.*

Upon theſe principles we may perhaps be able to give a more complete ſolution than hath hitherto been given of a paradox in the hiſtory of letters: viz. Why, gene-rally, the firſt regular compoſitions of any

O 2   people

people fhould be in *verfe*, rather than in *profe*. One reafon, no doubt, was that, antecedent to the ufe of letters, verfe was much more proper than profe in compofitions that were defigned to perpetuate the memory of remarkable tranfactions and events, as deviations from the original would be made with more difficulty, and corrupted paffages reftored with more eafe : But, additional to this, we may perhaps affirm with truth, that the concatenation of fentences is not fo intricate in verfe, as in profe. Not unfrequently the negleft of regular tranfitions is efteemed graceful in verfe and the old poems here referred to, as the *Delphin Oracles*, &c. where the fenfe was generally compleated in a line, or a fhort ftanza, required very little art or variety of connexion. How much more elaborate in point of tranfition and concatenation of fentences is even the hiftory

hiftory of *Herodotus* than the poems of *Homer*, many parts of which are hiftorical.

Another thing which *Grammarians* and writers attend to in fentences is the order of the words of which they confift. Of this fome languages admit of a much greater variety than others, owing to a difference in their original ftructure. When the relations of words to words are expreffed by terminations, it is a matter of indifference, with refpect to the fenfe, in what order the words ftand. Whereas in languages that do not denote the relations of words to one another by terminations, but do it in fome meafure by their place, the order of words is neceffarily limited and invariable. I fhall fubjoin an example.

Alexander vicit Darium, Alexander conquered Darius. Tranfpofe the *Latin*

words

words in every manner poffible, the fenfe is in no danger of being miftaken; but change the order of the words in the *Eng-lifh* tranflation, and the fenfe is either render-ed ambiguous, or is abfolutely contradictory.

Notwithftanding this reftriction, *Modern* languages admit of a confiderable liberty of tranfpofition in other refpects, in common with the *Antient*; for intire claufes of a fentence, which contain a whole circum-ftance of the affirmation, may be tranfpofed at pleafure, without endangering the fenfe or the perfpicuity: as if to the former fen-tence he added the circumftance of *three battles*, it is indifferent whether we fay, *Alexander conquered Darius in three battles. In three battles Alexander con-quered Darius, or Alexander in three bat-tles conquered Darius.*

But

But not only many a writer take the liberty to change the order of his words in a sentence; but, in most languages, every complex sentence is capable of a great variety of expression, by little more than a different construction of the same words; which contribute greatly to the ease and harmony of composition. I shall instance in the last mentioned sentence the sense of which may be expressed by saying either, that *Alexander conquered Darius*, or *Darius was conquered by Alexander*.

Further, by introducing other words of similar signification, as the mention of minute and slight circumstances, a sentence admits of still greater variety of expression. Thus we may say, *Three battles were fought and Darius was at the mercy of Alexander. Alexander fought three battles before he subdued Darius*, &c. &c.

Languages

Languages that have a great copia of words are much preferable to others on this account; since, by a small alteration of this kind, a writer may give what degree of emphasis or precision he pleases to an expression; in the command of which, the accuracy and excellency of style doth greatly consist.

In all languages that admit of the inflexions of words, care must be taken, with respect to the syntax, that the terminations do properly correspond. The rules respecting this are called rules of *concord*, and of *government*. Concord respects chiefly the agreement of the *substantive* with its *adjective*, when both are declined alike. In *Latin* and *Greek* it is necessary that they agree in number, case, and gender. For example *bonus puer* is good latin; but *bona*, *bonum*, *boni*, or *bono* puer are bad. In

English

English no care is neceſſary in this reſpect, ſince our adjectives have neither number, caſe, or gender: but *English* pronominal adjectives, which are in part declined, may, diſagree with their ſubſtantives: thus we muſt always write, *theſe books*, and not *this books*.

Government chiefly reſpects the putting the proper caſe after a verb: Thus, ſince, in Latin, verbs tranſitive regularly require an accuſative caſe after them, it is wrong to ſay *amo magiſtro*, and not *magiſtrum*.

The great variety there is in the conſtruction of languages, that admit of many inflexions of words, makes it difficult to learn, and eſpecially to uſe them.*(a)* The
Latin

(a) In languages that do not abound with inflections, it is neverthelefs remarkable how

Latin and *Greek* however, are not fo irregular in their fyntax as, at firft fight, they
feem to be: fince able Grammarians have
fhown that, by fupplying fuppofed ellipfes,
many of the moft irregular conftructions are
perfectly analogous to the moft ufual and
fimple ones, and have thereby reduced the
original rules of fyntax into a much fmaller
compafs than could well have been imagined.

Thus, for example, they have fhown
that thofe words which are commonly faid
to govern a genitive, do it by means of another noun underftood, to which it is the
latter;

differently words, and particularly pronouns in
conftruction are placed. And how aukward the
manner of one people would look, if it were
adopted by another: for inftance, if we would
render into *French* this expreffion. *I carry you
fome thither :* we muft fay, *Je vous y en porte ;*
which put in the fame order in *Engiifh*, is *I you
thither fome carry*.

latter; and every ablative is governed by a prepofition expreffed or underftood: for inftance in this fentence, *Eft fapientis*, the word *fapientis* is not properly governed of the verb *eft*, but is the latter of two nouns, of which *officium*, *ars*, or fome word of the like import is the former: and accordingly, the proper Englifh of it is. *It is the duty, or the part of a wife man.* In *fortior Alexandro, braver than Alexander*, *Alexandro* is governed by the prepofition *præ*, which is fuppreffed. In like manner may moft other irregular conftructions be accounted for.

LECTURE

LECTURE the TWELFTH,

OF THE

REGULAR GROWTH

AND

CORRUPTION.

OF

LANGUAGES.

LANGUAGES, like all other arts which owe their cultivation, if not their invention, to men, which fubfift by their ufe of them, and are daily fubject to human caprice, cannot be expected to continue long in the fame ftate: whether *ancient,*

ent, or *modern;* whether *simple*, or *complex* in their ftructure, they have a kind of *regular growth, improvement,* and *declenfion;* and are moreover liable to many *intermediate fluctuations.* No internal conftitution can preferve them either from the general revolutions, or the particular accidents.

The regular growth of languages proceeds from the neceffity of giving names to new objects, new ideas, and new combinations of ideas; combinations exifting, either in nature, or formed in the imagination. Hence the language of thofe nations hath ever grown copious whofe fituation and occafions were fuch as brought them acquainted with various fcenes of nature, or obliged them to have recourfe to the improvements of art.

The private life and policy of the *Hebrews*, living under an abfolute monarchy,

P   and

and whofe religion forbad them the ufe of
the arts of painting and ftatuary; and the
immediate defign of which was to keep them
clear of all connection with neighbouring
nations,(a) was too uniform to afford them
many opportunities or occafions of enlarging, or embellifhing their language.

Whereas the *Greeks*, divided into a great
number of feparate communities, perpetually vying with each other in power, policy,
commerce, and arts; moft of the ftates re-
publics, where all kind of honours and
emoluments were the prize of eloquence;
whofe private policy abounded with fuch
inftitutions as games, feftivals, &c. which
drew a vaft concourfe of people together,
and

(a) That was a means ufed to anfwer one
great defign of their conftitution, viz. preferving
them from idolatry.

and where men diftinguifhed themfelves by their talents in publick fpeaking; where not only publick confultations were held for the general utility of *Greece*, but poems, and even hiftories, were recited in publick, could not fail giving particular attention to their language. And *Athens*, whofe conftitution was a more perfect democracy, and in other refpects afforded more fcope for the ufe of language, and where the rewards of literary excellence were more certain, and more inviting, was deemed to be in a more efpecial manner the feat of eloquence in Greece. The Athenians in general valued themfelves upon their exquifite tafte for the purity and propriety of their language, and among them the arts of oratory were held in reputation, and flourifhed long after polite literature was totally forgotten in every other part of Greece.

Next

Next to the *Athenians*, the inhabitants
of the fea port towns of *Afia minor*, addicted to commerce, fubject to frequent revolutions, and peculiarly connected with
Athens, diftinguifhed themfelves for their
fkill in the powers of language.

Univerfally, in countries where there
were no arts to exercife the inventive facul-
ties of men, and to augment and diverfify
their ftock of ideas, nor any other induce-
ment to excel in the ufe of fpeech, language hath been very barren; and, in every
refpect, ill adapted to exprefs the ideas of
more cultivated minds. What the poems
were that *Ovid* wrote in the *Gctic* language
we are not informed; but certain we may
be, from the nature of things, that they
muft have fallen infinitely fhort of his
Latin compofitions; if not in delicacy of
fentiment,

fentiment, at leaft in accuracy and eafe of expreffion.

The progrefs of human life in general is from poverty to riches, and from riches to luxury, and ruin: in *Architecture* ftructures have always been at firft heavy, and inconvenient, then ufeful and ornamental, and laftly real propriety and magnificence have been loft in fuperfluous decorations. Our very *drefs* is at firft plain and aukward, then eafy and elegant, and laftly downright fantaftical. Stages of a fimilar nature may be obferved in the progrefs of all human arts; and language, being liable to the fame influences, hath undergone the fame changes. Whenever a language hath emerged from its firft rough ftate of nature, and hath acquired a fufficient copia of fignificant and harmonious terms, arbitrary and whimfical ideas of excellence have been

P 3 fuperadded

fuperadded to thofe which were natural and becoming, till at length the latter have been intirely facrificed to the former.

I fhall exemplify thefe obfervations by a fhort hiftory of the revolutions of the *Roman* language. About the time of the firft *Punic* war, when the infcription upon the *Columna Roftra* was written, the Latin tongue feems to have been very barbarous, and void of that regularity and harmony which it was afterwards diftinguifhed by. In confequence of more extenfive connections with foreign countries and ftates, in confequence of the Romans having more power, wealth, and influence to contend for among themfelves, and efpecially upon the introduction of the Grecian arts and fciences, all the chief men of the ftate applied themfelves with indefatigable affiduity to the cultivation of their language, and

and in one age it arrived to all the perfection it ever attained.

In this ftate it continued till the diffolution
of the commonwealth; after which time when
little ufe was made of the Roftrum, and
judicial proceedings took a form which left
little to the pleader: when, in fhort, the
practice of oratory did not bring along with
it thofe honours and advantages that had
formerly attended it; in thofe circumftances, perfons addicted to letters having no
occafion for the ancient manly and free
eloquence, fell, through an affectation of
novelty, into a number trifling and puerile
refinements in ftyle: analogies, inftead of
being fetched from nature, were borrowed
from language itfelf; and verbal conceits
and turns were admired for true wit and
juft fentiment. Afterwards, upon the irruption of the northern barbarians, the language

guage itfelf became mixed and adulterated
as well as the tafte of the writers corrupted:
univerfal confufion was introduced, and the
old *Roman* tongue intirely loft.

There are certain limits beyond which the
growth of a language cannot extend.
Whatever be the improvements in human
life, and the human mind; let men's acquaintance with the powers of nature and
art be ever fo extenfive, their ideas and thofe
combinations and relations of them which it
will be at all convenient to exprefs by words
cannot be infinite. When, therefore, a people hath words and modifications of words fufficient for the occafions they have for the ufe
of them, for the language to grow ftill more
copious, and to have words and modifications
to exprefs more things and relations than
they could attend to, were abfurd and bur-
thenfome.   Trees, in the moft proper foil
and

and climate, grow but to a certain height; and when arrived to their full fize, all the redundant juices ferve only to nourifh various excrefcences, as funguffes, moffes, &c. which deform and wafte them.   In like manner, all the pains that we beftow upon a language, when it is fufficiently perfect for all the ufes of it, ferve only to disfigure it, to leffen its real value, and incumber it with ufelefs rules and refinements, which embarrafs the fpeaker or writer, and are of no advantage to the hearer or reader.

The time in which a language arrives at its perfection, it is natural to conjecture, will be when the people that fpeak it have occafion to make the greateft ufe of it; which will be when their power and influence abroad, and when arts, fciences and liberty at home are at the greateft height.   As thefe grow lefs confiderable, the language will
naturally

naturally contract itself with the occasions of it, if it be not preserved by writing.

When a language is complete in all its parts, and the Grammar of it hath received its last improvement, the introduction of a few new terms, suited to casual new ideas and occurrences, and adjusted to the established rules, doth not deserve the name of an improvement in the language.   We do not call an oak, that is grown to its full size, more perfect, for an additional leaf or acorn.   Perhaps one intire century favourable to the polite arts may have been sufficient, in general, to bring any language to its perfection.

Before a language have acquired a sufficient number of modifications and forms of speech, different forms must necessarily be adopted by different persons: but the best

forms

forms of fpeech, the moft commodious for ufe, and the moft agreeable to the analogy of the language, will at length eftablifh themfelves, and become univerfal, by their fuperior excellence: and at the time that a language hath begun to be fpoken and written with uniformity, it may be taken for granted, to be arrived to its maturity and perfection. For till a fufficient number of forms have become univerfal, different forms will occur to different perfons, and the language will be written with great diffimilarity. The *Englifh* language, in particular, cannot be faid to have been fixed till about the reign of queen *Ann.* Before that time, every writer adopted what words he thought proper from foreign tongues; only a fmall part of them have fince that period been in ufe: but they are now perfectly incorporated with the language, and our moft licenti-

ous

ous writers of any reputation are very fpar-
ing in introducing others.

In general, thofe writings which have
contributed to fix a language are deemed
claffical in a country, and a ftudied imitation
of them by fucceeding writers tends ftill
more to promote a perfect uniformity in
writing.

The progrefs of a language towards perfection may be confiderably accelerated by
the labours of perfons who give their attention to it; if they ftudy the analogy of the
language, recommend phrafes that are a-
greeable to it, and detect and expofe thofe
that are improper. While literary critics
keep within thefe bounds, and their opinions
are left to recommend themfelves by their
own weight, they do a very important fervice to a language: but when their decifions
have

have the fanction of any authority, and forms of fpeech are adopted becaufe recom-mended by them, and not on account of the reafons that might be alledged in their favour, fince all men, and all bodies of men, are fallible, the interpofition of their autho-rity is in danger of contributing to eftablifh phrafes and conftructions, which the more mature judgment of after ages would fee reafon to correct: and though the fpirit of men will affert their liberty, in rejecting what they do not approve, fuch undue influence may keep a language much longer in an imperfect ftate than it otherwife would have been.

All the real fervice that any men, or bodies of men, can do to a language, is to analyze it into its parts, to fhow diftinctly what are the materials and compofition of it, and thereby make the whole ftructure

Q   of

of it perfectly underftood. For when, by the judicious difpofition of every thing belonging to a language, all its analogies are feen at one view, it will prefently appear what is redundant, deficient, or ambiguous, in the words or conftruction of it.

Before an improvement can be made of any thing its prefent powers muft be perfectly known. Before we can improve upon *Nature*, by an artificial combination of its powers, the laws of nature muft be underftood; and they are only to be underftood by a careful obfervation of what doth in fact take place in confequence of them. A digeft of thefe obfervations makes a fyftem of natural philofophy.

In like manner, to improve upon a language, obfervations muft be made upon the manner in which words are actually ufed in
it

it. A methodical enumeration of the rules and laws of its conftruction is the *Grammar* of it; as a *Dictionary* is that which contains all the words of a language, and an account of all the fenfes in which they are ufed. If the language be a dead one, the remains only of the writers of it can be made ufe of; if it be a living one, the forms of converfation muft not be wholly overlooked, In the former cafe, no innovations can be made. Thofe who wrote in the language while it was a living one will be accounted the ftandards of it, and even their imperfections muft be adopted by all who ufe it after them; unlefs (as hath been thought of with refpect to fome of the dead languages) mankind fhould agree to form a more perfect and philofophical language out of the remains of it: in which cafe, it could no longer be confidered as a dead, but as a revived and living language.

Q 2

In

In modern and living languages, it is abfurd to pretend to fet up the compofitions of any perfon or perfons whatfoever as the ftandard of writing, or their converfation as the invariable rule of fpeaking. With refpect to cuftoms, laws, and every thing that is changeable, the body of a people, who, in this refpect, cannot but be free, will certainly affert their liberty, in making what innovations they judge to be expedient and ufeful. The general prevailing cuftom, where ever it happen to be, can be the only ftandard for the time that it prevails. And in a cafe that admits of no authority to controul a man's actions, it is in vain to pretend that any perfon may not attempt to introduce whatever he thinks to be an improvement. Indeed the fear of becoming ridiculous is fufficient to prevent, many very extravagant and abfurd propofals.

The

The chief thing to be attended to in the improvement of a language is the *analogy* of it. The more confiftent are its principles, the more it is of a piece with itfelf, the more commodious it will be for ufe: and it cannot be looked upon as any great or a-larming innovation, meerly to difufe fome conftructions that clafh with others, and to confine ones felf to one fenfe of any fingle word or phrafe.

That immenfe and valuable performance of Mr. *Johnfon's* contains an account of al-moft all the fenfes in which all the words of the Englifh language are ufed: and it is very poffible, from little more than the ex-amples he hath given from our beft writers of the ufe of every word in every fenfe, to compofe a grammar of all the varieties of manner in which words are ufed, both as to their inflection and difpofition, which, toge-

Q 3   ther

ther with the dictionary, would be a complete fyftem of our language as now ufed.

Merely to drop what, from a view of fuch a fyftem, were apparently ufelefs and inconvenient, would make the language as perfect as the general nature of it would admit. To introduce into it all that, upon the fame view, would appear to be wanting to it, might feem too great an innovation; to alter its nature, and character, and make another language: and if it were thought neceffary to form a new language, it were better to begin from the firft, upon the moft philofophical principles, than take for the foundation of it any of the imperfect languages now in ufe.

LECTURE

LECTURE the THIRTEENTH.

OF THE

COMPLEX STRUCTURE

OF THE

GREEK AND LATIN

LANGUAGES.

TO a perfon who confidereth the plainnefs and fimplicity of all infant arts, it muft appear extremely improbable that the *Greek* and *Latin* languages (and the fame may be faid, in fome degree, of the

Arabick,

Arabick, and others of which some account hath been given) should have been so complex in their primitive structure as they appear to be in the Greek and Roman classics. With respect to the Greek in particular (which may be stiled the mother of the Latin tongue) What occasion, it may be asked, had a few tribes of wandering *Cimmerians (a)* (for the first inhabitants of *Greece* were nothing more) for a language so overstocked with *cases, declensions, genders, conjugations, tenses, moods,* &c. These are evidently superfluous to human converse, and can it be supposed that a people, who had barely

(a) If we suppose the language we now call *Greek* not to have been that which was spoken by the original inhabitants of *Greece* but that the rudiments of it at least were introduced by *Egyptian* or other eastern colonies, we only transfer the difficulty, and leave it to be enquired how the language of those new comers grew to be so complex.

barely the neceſſaries of life, ſhould abound in the ſuperfluities of language.

It is, moreover, obſervable that languages do not neceſſarily grow more complex in their ſtructure, in conſequence of their improvement in the copia of words, harmony, preciſion, or any other real excellence. The *Engliſh* language in its preſent ſtate is certainly a great improvement upon the ancient *Saxon:* yet ſo far have we been from adopting any new inflections of words; that we have, without any manner of inconvenience, dropped the greater part of thoſe they had.

It may therefore be enquired how a language, having, at firſt, no more than neceſſary inflections (if any inflections may be called neceſſary) ſhould acquire ſo many more than are neceſſary: and why all languages

guages in their progress from simplicity to refinement should not go through the same stages; but that some, as they become more perfect, should grow more simple, while others grow more complex.

In an attempt to solve so curious a problem, and account for so remarkable a fact, it may not be unpleasing to observe, to how small a difference in the first principles of languages it might be owing that, in their progress, they came to be so unlike one another.

To recur to the principles laid down in the fourth lecture: All the necessary words of a language are either the names of things, or words contrived to express the relations of these to one another; which are called auxiliary words. Two languages may consist of the same words, that is, the people that

use

ufe them may call every thing by the fame name, but have a quite different manner of expreffing their relations; or, on the contrary, their manner of ufing words may be the fame, but the words themfelves be totally different. In this latter cafe, the ftructure or genius of the languages is faid to be the fame, and the Gran.mar of them muft be precifely the fame: whereas, in the former cafe, though the fame words or names of things were ufed, the different manner of ufing them would make the grammar rules of the two languages quite different. The one might be extremely fimple, and the other complex: a very few inftructions might explain every thing relating to one of the languages, exclufive of what was contained in the dictionary of it; but to have the dictionary of the other by heart might not be to have half learned it.

The

The methods of expreſſing the relations of words to words are principally two: the one is by the inflection of them, that is ſome change in the form of them; and the other by auxiliary words, appropriated to the ſeveral relations: ſometimes alſo re-courſe is had to bare poſition.

It is not the uſe of one or the other of the two former methods, in themſelves con-ſidered, that neceſſarily renders the ſtructure of one language more complex than that of another. There is ſomething new to be at-tended to in both: and what is the difference whether that be a new termination or the junction of a new word with it? The ſame change of termination and the ſame auxili-ary word, were they made uſe of invariably to expreſs the ſame relation, would be learned with the ſame eaſe, for example, what greater difficulty wou'd it be to remem-

ber

ber that that the relation we intend by the genitive cafe of the word *Carthago*, *Carthage*, were made by *Carthaginis* as in Latin; or *of Carthage*, as in Englifh: or can it be faid that the change of *amo* to *amaveram*, or of *love* to *had loved* is either of them a greater burden to the memory than the other? In like manner were all the words of the moft extenfively inflected language inflected with perfect regularity, it would not, in reality, be more complex in confequence of it.

The advantage of a language which makes ufe of auxiliary words above another which hath recourfe to inflection, in point of fimplicity, is owing to this; that auxiliary words are of univerfal application, and do very rarely either affect, or are affected by, the cafual form of the word they are annexed to; Whereas it was never found that the

R   fame

fame inflections would equally fuit all words
of the fame kind. And fince, in giving
names to things, no regard could be paid to
uniformity of termination, words that muft
be ufed in the fame relations muft be inflected differently, to exprefs them; according to the difference in the original form of
the word: and this being prodigioufly various,
it hath occafioned, in fome languages, fuch
variety of inflections as makes the grammar
of them extremely intricate.

As to the pofition of words in different
languages, though in fact it be feldom quite
arbitrary; it is (except in a few cafes) a thing
that is regulated rather by an attention to
harmony, or conformity to cuftom, than a
matter of abfolute neceffity.

Now confidering that no people would
make their language complex by defign
(for

(for it cannot be suppofed but that thofe peculiar advantages of the Greek and Roman tongues which they derive from their being complex, were accidental, with refpect to them, and not perceived till long after the languages were formed) we muft have recourfe in part to accident, and in part to neceffity to account for it.

I et us now fuppofe that the people who firft fpoke the principal Northern tongues had their organs fo formed, or that it fo happened by accident, that they did not give the air a free paffage out of their mouths, but made great ufe of their tongues and lips in retarding and modulating it : which would produce a great proportion of confonants in their words; and that the people who firft fpoke the Greek language were led by oppofite caufes to introduce a greater proportion of vowels into their primitive

words.

words.   This fingle circumftance would
make it eafy to change or add to the terminations of Greek words: for the words generally ending either in a vowel, or a fingle
confonant, any addition might be made to
them, without a fenfible hiatus, or inter-
ruption of the breath; which could not but
often be the confequence of attempting to
make an addition to the terminations of
words in the Northern tongues.

Let us likewife confider that, fince no
people would invent new words without neceffity, it would be the moft natural for all
people to begin to exprefs variations in the
ufe of words, by alterations in the words
themfelves; and that the nature of auxiliary
words is founded on more abftract and me-
taphyfical ideas;   as the attempt to define
them will fhow.   The method of inflection
therefore was firft made ufe of by all nations,

ons, as the moſt natural; and the Greek language would eaſily admit the continuance of it to a very great degree. Whereas thoſe people who uſed the northern tongues were not able to go much further in it than a few of the moſt common and familiar affections of words: for the reſt they were obliged to make uſe of auxiliary words. But that the method of inflection is the moſt natural appears to be further evident from this fact, that the moſt common words of all languages, and the moſt common relations of words are the firſt in which inflections take place, and the laſt in which they are exterminated; as in the ſecond and third perſons ſingular of verbs, the three perſonal pronouns, the plural numbers of nouns, &c.

But it ſeldom happens that that which is firſt in order of time and nature, is likewiſe firſt in real excellence and perfection.

Picture-

Picture-writing was, undoubtedly, more natural than alphabetical, and antecedent to it;
but, notwithftanding, far inferior. And
had the Greeks been aware of the extenfive
ufe and convenience of auxiliary words, they
would certainly not have made fo great ufe
of inflections. But happening in the firft
rudiments of their language to have no occafion for words correfponding to our *fhall*,
will, *may*, *muft*, *have*, &c. having no
words to exprefs what we mean by *to*, *for*,
&c. and, whether through an affectation of
brevity, or inattention, not repeating the
perfonal pronouns with verbs, they were
under an abfolute neceffity of inflecting their
words according to what Grammarians call
the *cafes* of nouns, and the *tenfes*, *moods*,
and *perfons* of verbs; and, to have made
their language perfect upon that plan, they
ought to have proceeded much further in
inflections than they actually did: even till
the

the Grammar of the language had been as complex as the Chinefe method of writing.

The particulars above mentioned for the radical difference between the ftructure of a language like the Greek, and a language like ours: and from thefe it is eafy to fee how all the other particulars in which they differed from us followed of courfe.

As the Greeks could not but pay fome attention to the analogy of the forms of their words, and perceive that all their nouns and verbs did not terminate alike, and had every other difference that the names of things and actions affixed at random could not but have; they would find it aukward, and even impoffible, to inflect them alike: hence arofe the arbitrary diftinction of *declenfions* of nouns, and *conjugations* of verbs,

verbs, depending on the cafual form of the words.

For the fame reafon that nouns fubftantive were inflected, though not with the fame neceffity, adjectives becaufe they are fometimes ufed without their fubftantives were inflected too, and, that they might correfpond to one another, it was moft convenient to inflect them in a fimilar manner.

Nature having evidently made a diftinction of fex in many things to which men gave names, and the names of the different fexes differing generally, for obvious reafons, in termination only: as *equus, equa: leo, leæna (a)* they began, agreeable to the fame analogy,

(a) I make ufe of illuftrations from the *Latin* tongue, becaufe they will be the moft generally underftood.

analogy, to vary the termination of the cor-
refpondent adjectives according to it, and to
fay *bonus equus, bona equa.* Thus they
became poffeffed of a *mafculine* and *feminine
gender,* both in fubftantives and adjectives.

Purfuing the fame analogy, they made a
neuter gender, at firft, moft probably, for
thofe things, in which it would have been
abfurd to imagine any diftinction of fex; as
mare the fea, *cælum* heaven, *faxum* a ftone,
&c. and had they purfued this analogy
ftrictly, and claffed every thing elfe that
had no fex among the neuters, the diftinction, though unneceffary, would have been
natural and confiftent: But dropping the
analogy of nature, a mere fancied analogy
to a fex, or an analogy of the terminations
of words to thofe of others, which, on account of their fex, were before made mafculine or feminine, determined them to
rank

rank others among the mafculines and feminines, which a ftrict adherence to nature
would have excluded from either clafs.

Thus, for example, the fun having a
ftronger, and the moon a weaker influence
over the world, and there being but two
celeftial bodies fo remarkable, all nations,
I believe, that ufe genders have afcribed to
the fun the gender of the male, and to the
moon that of the female. To illuftrate the
analogy of termination, it having happened
that the names of many malas ended in *us*,
for inftance, and of their correfponding fe-
males in *a*, many other nouns ending in
us, as *murus*, were, by the analogy of termination, made mafculine, and inflected like
them; and, for the fame reafon, many o-
ther nouns ending in *a*, as *aqua*, became
feminines.

There

There being two diſtinct reaſons for af-
fixing the genders of words, ſo different as
of ſignification and termination, it could not
but happen that, in ſuch a prodigious variety of names, and terminations of words
given at random, they muſt ſometimes interfere; the ſignification ſometimes occaſioning a difference of gender in the ſame termination; and, at other times, the termination occaſioning a difference of gender when
the ſignification was the ſame.

LECTURE

LECTURE the FOURTEENTH.

THE

SAME SUBJECT

CONTINUED.

ANOTHER fource of different inflections, particularly in the tenfes of
verbs, was probably accident, and neither
neceffity nor analogy, viz. the fame radical
word happening to be inflected differently
by different perfons, and different tribes of
a nation at the fame time. Thefe modifications though fuggefted by the fame neceffity of expreffing the fame new relations
and

and circumſtances, and therefore having the ſame ſignification) becoming generally known, and uſed at firſt promiſcuouſly, would neceſſarily, in time, be uſed, in different ſenſes, as far as the nature of the thing would admit.

This may be illuſtrated by a very late and parallel inſtance in our own tongue. Not long ago the words *be* and *am* were uſed preciſely in the ſame ſenſe, and promiſcuouſly : but now all accurate writers apply them in a different manner, uſing *am* in a poſitive aſſertion, as *I am;* and *be* where there is any uncertainty in the event; as, *if I be.* Though very frequently in converſation, and particularly in ſome counties, we ſtill hear theſe words confounded.

In this manner might the Greek *perfects,* *futures,* and *aoriſts,* and many of the tenſes

S   of

of the *middle voice* have been invented, at firſt by different tribes of the numerous un-connected ſtates of **Greece**, then have ſpread, and for ſome time have been uſed promiſcu-ouſly; and laſtly with as much difference as the nature of things would admit of.   In-deed at laſt the varieties of inflection exhauſt-ed the diſtinctions of nature. *(a)*

It requires no words to explain in what manner the *Syntax* of the Greek and Latin languages became ſo complex, it being the immediate and neceſſary conſequence of a multiplicity of inflections.

This

(a) In theſe obſervations I have had the *Greek* language chiefly in view.   The *Latin* inflecti-ons are little more than an imperfect imitation of the Greek, and the manner of their deriva-tion from the Greek is ſimilar to the derivation of the modern Greek from it, and that of ſome modern European tongues from the Latin,

This multiplicity of inflections could only be formed while the language was in its infancy, before it was fixed, and while, upon the plan they set out with, there was a necessity of inventing new modifications of words. For it is perhaps impossible to assign a single instance of any language gaining new inflections after it became fixed, and reduced to any kind of standard, though never so imperfectly, by writing; or, perhaps, after it was spoken with tolerable uniformity by the people who used it.

The *Greeks* added nothing to the structure of their language after the times of *Homer;* to whom likewise it probably descended unaltered from their earliest poets. The *Romans*, after they became acquainted with the Grecian language, and arts, (which was a means of perfecting their own) added not a single mood or tense in imitati-

S 2   on

on of the Greek; though the fimilarity of
the two languages would have made it very
practicable.   The remains of the *Latin*
tongue fpoken in *Italy*, *France*, and *Spain*,
have not borrowed a fingle inflection from
the original Latin, fince its revival in the
weft, when thofe languages were very imperfect, and men of learning generally made
ufe of the Latin in preference to them.
Laftly, the *Englifh*, as was obferved before,
inftead of enlarging and perfecting the cafes
and declenfions of their *Saxon* mother
tongue, hath almoft dropped them all.

There is, therefore, no reafon in the
world to believe that any language will ever
acquire more inflections, and grow more
complex, through the choice of thofe who
ufe it.   It is with languages as with all cuftoms and habits; when they are fixed they
are not eafily changed.   Who would chufe
to

to introduce new words, or new modifications of words, when they found no new purpofes which the old ones might not be
made to anfwer?

It is obfervable that even the moft polifhed nations have ever been the moft backward to admit any alteration in whatever re-
lates to language, efpecially in whatever
comes near the foundation of it. Were not
the *Athenians* the laft to admit the new
letters introduced after the time of *Cadmus*?
Are not the learned men of every modern
European nation convinced that both the
Alphabets and Grammars of their refpective
languages might be greatly improved, and
yet what fuccefs have the attempts of ingenious men to make innovations met with?

The advantages and difadvantages of inflections and auxiliary words in languages

S 3   may

may be illustrated by the use of *arbitrary characters* representing ideas, as the Chinese, also some that are used in books of short hand, and an *alphabet of letters*, which represent sounds. To a certain degree, arbitrary characters, by being shorter, may be more convenient than characters representing words; as particularly in the nine digits: but, continued beyond that degree, (as they are in a great measure independent, and unconnected) they become more burdensome to the memory than the use of a regular alphabet; which, though perhaps more tedious in writing single words, is easily varied, and is as intelligible in the new as in old combinations.

In like manner, a few inflections, (one particularly to distinguish the plural number from the singular) may prevent tedious periphrases; but if we regard the circumstan-

ces

ces of mankind, we fhould not multiply thefe concife forms of fpeech till the rules of a language bear too great a proportion to the abilities and leifure of the people who are to ufe it.

Auxiliary words bring the rules, or Grammar, of a language into a fmall compafs; whereby they are the more eafily obferved, and give a language a fairer chance of being perpetuated. It feems to be naturally impoffible that the Greek and Roman tongues fhould have been fpoken, in their full extent and purity, except by fcholars and philofophers: to the common people a great number of their inflections muft, of neceffity, have been ufelefs or ambiguous: Whereas the fimplicity of the *Englifh* makes it eafy to be fpoken in its purity by all who ufe it, and have been inftructed in the few rules of it, and bids fair for preferving
ing

ing it unchanged to the lateſt ages.   This
will appear more diſtinctly when we conſider the cauſes and manner of the corrup-
tion of an inflected language.

Having endeavoured to ſhow in what manner ſuch complex languages,   as the Greek
and Latin, are originally formed, and given
a general idea of the convenience or inconvenience of them;   I ſhall, in laſt place,
conſider in what manner they gradually
break, and particularly in what manner the
ancient *Greek* ſunk into the *modern*, and the
ancient *Latin* into *Italian*, *French*, and
Spaniſh.

I muſt premiſe that, in theſe ſpeculations,
a good deal muſt be left to conjecture, ſince
it is not very eaſy to trace the changes of a
cultivated language in its progreſs to a ſtate
of barbariſm;   though it be extremely eaſy

to

to trace a barbarous langnage to a ftate of perfection. 'The reafon is that all authors are ambitious of writing according to the pureft ftandard of the language they make ufe of. In the introductions to almoft all our Englifh dictionaries, we fee every ftage of the changes of the *Saxon* tongue, down to the modern *Englifh;* but in *Latin*, we have nothing intermediate between what (in the view in which we now confider the language) may be called *claffical*, and the modern *Italian*, *French*, and *Spanifh;* nor between the ancient *Greek* and that which is now fpoken in *Turkey in Europe*. The The variations muft have amounted to a new language before they would, knowingly, be adopted by writers in general.

No perfons but thofe who underftood the old language would be qualified to be writers; and, before the art of printing, very

few

few books were written for the ufe of the common people. Sometime after the revival of letters in Europe, men of learning wrote chiefly for the perufal of men of learning. It is only in the accidental prefervation of vulgar fayings, fuch as *acclamations*, *fongs*, *proverbs*, &c. few of which remain in Greek and Latin, that the intermediate ftate of a language, between its perfection and imperfect reftauration appears.

Every complex language muft neceffarily grow lefs fo when the people who ufe it want leifure to learn and attend to all the minute diftinctions of it, and they find they can be underftood by methods which are eafier and more fimple. Thus we may take it for granted that, in the confufion of the Greek and Roman affairs, as the people, in their manners, cuftoms, &c. relapfed by degrees into their former barbarity; the elegancies,

gancies, refinements, and fuperfluities of
their language were difufed, and they were
content with making themfelves underftood
by the help of fewer inflections than remain
in their beft writers.

But the prefent *Italian*, *French* and
Spanish tongues, moft probably, took their
rife from the imperfect attempts of barbarous nations to fpeak the Roman tongue,
and particularly in the provinces; and that
long before the diffolution of the Roman
empire by the irruption of the northern
nations.

If we confider the Grammar of thofe
languages with attention and compare them
with the Latin, we may almoft fee the
very manner in which they were produced.
Foreign nations, in attempting to fpeak
Latin, could not avoid imitating the principal

pal tenfes of their verbs: accordingly we can plainly difcern the form of them in their prefent languages. When people who had not the advantage of a regular and perfect inftruction endeavoured to fpeak in Latin, they would naturally think of nothing but of rendering the words of their own tongue literally into it; and when nations of the *Teutonic* original had rendered into fome fort of Latin, or retained, their own articles, cafual prepofitions, and auxiliary words (which, being fundamental in their own language, would be the laft things they would part with, and indeed what they could have no idea of their being able to do without) they would find that more in-flections were unneceffary. The Roman foldiers, who formed the colonies, being no great mafters of the language, would make no great difficulty of leaning to this barbarous manner of fpeaking it. It

confirms

confirms this conjecture, that the present *Italian*, *French*, and *Spanish* tongues were originally called *Roman*, in opposition to the native languages of those who spoke them.

Greece being continually open to the inroads of the *Italians*, *Germans*, *French*, and other northern *Europeans*; particularly about the time of the *Croisades*, the *Greek* language admitted a good deal of the idiom of the northern tongues in the same manner: though, from the forementioned internal causes, it had lost a great number of its inflections before; as was most observable about the time of the emperor *Justinian*, and this change had begun so early as the translation of the seat of the empire from *Rome* to *Constantinople*.

In the *modern Greek*, we see almost a

T

literal

literal tranflation of fome of the Teutonic
auxiliary verbs into Greek, in   for
had, and   for will; which of courfe
fupplanted a great part of their former variety of tenfes; for the modern Greeks fay

I had written,

thou hadft written, &c.

I will write,

Thou wilt write, &c. and to fupply the
place of moods, they have evidently tranflated their own forms of expreffing the
modes of affirmation into Greek particles,
which they have prefixed to the common
inflections.

LECTURE

LECTURE the FIFTEENTH,

OF THE

REVOLUTIONS

OF

LANGUAGES

AND OF

TRANSLATION.

LANGUAGES would never be loſt, were the People that ſpeak them ſuffered to continue perfectly unmixed with other nations: but they are liable to become

T 2 corrupt

corrupt and extinct by the influence of other languages, in various ways and degrees.

A language may be wholly loſt in a very ſhort time, if the people that ſpeak it be ſubdued and carried captive by a nation that ſpeaks a different language, and eſpecially if the captives be intermixed with the conquerors. Thus the *Jews* are ſaid to have loſt their language at the time of the *Babyloniſh captivity:* for after that time pure *Hebrew* remained only in the ſacred books, and the modern *Jews*, who have no liberal education, ſpeak no other language than that of the country they are born in.

A people having a dependance upon, and intercourſe with, another people, more conſiderable than themſelves, are in danger of exchanging their language, in time, for that of their powerful and more learned neighbours

bours. Thus the *English* seems to gain ground upon the *Welch*, and it may be supposed the *French* upon the *Britannoise*.

Neighbouring independent nations, speaking different languages, but having an intercourse with one another, cannot avoid borrowing words from one another: and the language of the contiguous boundaries must be a mixture of both.

One nation making an irruption into the country of another, and remaining with the inhabitants will, in some degree, introduce their language with themselves.

If the conquered nations be entirely destroyed, banished, or inslaved, their language will be wholly lost in the country. In consequence of one intire conquest, the ancient *British* language gave place to that

T 3   of

of their *Saxon* conquerors in England, and became confined to *Wales*.

If the conquerors be numerous, and intimately mixed with the old inhabitants, the ancient language may undergo a very confiderable alteration, not only in the change of its words, but in the very genius and conftitution of it.   Thus the people of *Italy*, in confequence of the frequent irruptions of the northern barbarians, have entirely changed their language, for another of a quite different genius and conftitution, with different laws of the modifications of words, and a different fyntax.

The *French* and *Spanifh*, but particularly the latter, have had the very frame of their language confiderably altered by the long refidence of the *Romans* among them: whereas *Britain*, being a later, and more diftant

diftant province of the empire, though it received almoft as many Latin words as any
neighbouring nation, did not change the
frame of its language in the leaft. The
Welch have many *Latin* words though not
fo many as the *Englifh* (who received a
great part of theirs through the medium of
the *Norman French*) but neither of the
languages have Latin terminations, Latin
declenfions, Latin conjugations, or a Latin
fyntax.

For the conftitution of a language is as
different a thing from the words of it as the
conftitution or form of government, in any
country, is different from the inhabitants of
it. For as, in the one, the people may all
change, and the laws and form of government remain the fame; fo a people may
change almoft all their words for others,
but make the new ones conform ftrictly to
the

the difpofition, and all the modifications of the old. Thus the *Latin* word *animal* is transferred without variation into *Englifh;* but it hath not carried along with it its cafes, *animalis, animali,* &c. and the Englifh plural is *animals,* not *animalia.*

A polifhed nation conquered by Barbarians hath generally infpired their favage conquerors with a love for their fciences; which being to be learned only in the language of the conquered people, it hath, on that account, recommended itfelf to the ftudy of the conquerors. Thus the *Greek* Language became familiar at *Rome* after the conqueft of *Greece* by the *Romans,*

When a cultivated language ceafes to be fpoken, it may reman in books, and when the introduction of the fciences into other countries makes thofe books to be fought after,

after, and the language, in some sense, to
revive, the only standard of that language
is the practice of those original authors:
whatever their practice will warrant, it is
allowed, may be imitated: but every word
or phrase that is not found in some original
author (though so far analogous to the genius of the language as to be in no danger of
being mistaken by those who are versed in
it) is by some condemned as barbarous, because it is uncertain whether the people
who spoke the language would have used it.

It seems, however, very possible to carry
our scrupulosity too far in this case, if we
consider the real uses of reviving a dead language. *Latin*, though a dead language, is
now, for the purpose of literature, and the
correspondence of the learned, revived in
Europe; being not only generally read, but
also written by all who pretend to a learned

or

or liberal education. Now it feems to be fufficient for our purpofe if the phrafes and conftructions we make ufe of be fuch as cannot be directly proved to be contrary to the practice of the ancients, though it be impoffible to find the very words, phrafes, or conftructions in any ancient writer. For though it be poffible the ancients might laugh at our modern Latin ftyle, we do not write for their perufal, and we are in no danger of giving the fame offence to thofe for whofe ufe we do write. Allowed forms of fpeech have no natural, but only an arbitrary preference to thofe which are difallowed. In language every thing is regulated by mere cuftom, and in things that have no internal excellence, we fhould confider only the ufes to which they are applied.

The tranflation of the ancient *Greek* and *Latin claffics* into modern lauguages is of prodigious

prodigious fervice to improve thofe languages: for the *Moderns*, endeavouring to
exprefs the fentiments of the *Ancients* with
exactnefs, will enlarge their own ftock of
words, and fix and afcertain their meaning
with the fame precifion. At prefent, with refpect to the *Greek* and *Latin* claffics, it is in a
manner the teft of the culture and excellence of modern languages to have good
tranflations of them, and the language of
any *Europeans* is reckoned barbarous and
unfinifhed till they have attempted and fuc-
ceeded in fuch tranflations.

As the chief difficulty of tranflation confifts
in rendering the idioms properly, I fhall in
this place confider the nature of them.

There are few words, in any language,
that are not made ufe of to exprefs more
ideas than one; and not only fuch as are
analogous

analogous to one another, as the *foot* of a man, the *foot* of a beaſt, the *foot* of a chair, the *foot* of a mouutain, &c. but ideas that have no ſort of reſemblance natural or artificial: as *bear* to carry a burden, and *bear* a beaſt. Now as languages were formed independant of one another, it cannot be ſuppoſed that any two terms ſhould denote a conſiderable number of the very ſame independant ideas; but that, though it may happen that, in ſeveral ſenſes, the words might be truly rendered the one by the other, the coincidence could hardly be ſo perfect, as that, in every circumſtance and connection, they ſhould convey the very ſame idea. Thus the *Romans* ſaid *cornua tauri*, and we ſay the *horns of a bull*; but though the *Romans* moreover ſaid *cornua exercitus*, we do not therefore ſay the *horns of an army*; but, uſing another metaphor, not at all more natural, but what cuſtom hath

hath eſtabliſhed, ſay the *wings of an army.*
Where, therefore, the coincidence doth not
hold, a tranſlator muſt be obliged to have
recourſe to different terms in his own language, to expreſs ideas for which the ſame
term ſuffices in the language he is tranſlat-
ing from.

Further, many of our compound ideas
are not natural, but artificial and arbitrary
combinations of ſimple ideas; particularly
thoſe of meaſures, cuſtoms, terms of art,
and thoſe relating to all the abſtract ſciences
in general. In theſe caſes, the occaſions and
circumſtances of people who ſpoke different
languages might be different, and not lead
them to form the ſame combinations; ſo that
one nation, not having the ſame ideas with
the other, but ideas conſiſting of different
parts, it is impoſſible they ſhould have terms
to expreſs them; as the *talents* of different

U   nations,

nations, the *oftracifm* of the *Athenians*, and
the *Levirate* among the *Jews*.

A tranflator from languages which contain fuch terms as thefe, namely fuch as reprefent combinations of ideas that were
never made in his own country, and for
which, therefore, he can find no names in
his own language, muft either treat them
as proper names, by adopting the very words
which are ufed in the languagehe is tranflating from, or form a new word from thofe
in his own language, which come the near-
eft to the foreign ideas that he would reprefent: and without the one or the other method it is impoffible to tranflate faithfully,
or indeed at all.

In all languages, likewife, fuch fenfes
are affixed to combinations of words as could
not be gathered from the component parts
of

of them; much lefs therefore will they bear
to be tranflated into thofe words in another
language, which generally anfwer to thofe
component parts. Of this kind is the phrafe
il y a, there is in *French*, the joint meaning
of which words could not be gathered from
the meaning of them feparately taken.
How abfurd would it be to render this
phrafe in *Englifh*, by *it hath there.*

In this cafe, intire words refemble
fingle letters in other words: that is, they
have no meaning in themfelves, but the
phrafe compofed out of them is the leaft
fignificant part into which the fentence it
helps to form can be divided; as, in general,
fingle words are the leaft fignificant parts of
a fentence.

Thefe complex kind of idioms are little
attended to by thofe who fpeak a language;

U 2   becaufe,

becaufe, from their infancy, they learn to affix fingle ideas to thofe whole fentences, in the fame manner as they ufually do to fingle words: for inftance how few *Englifh* people are aware that *to give over a thing* is an idiom of this kind, or a phrafe, of which the ideas of the parts do not compofe the idea of the whole; yet it requires but little reflection to make them fenfible of it.

When fuch idioms as thefe occur in tran-flating from one language to another, a tranflator muft do what the people who ufe it conftantly do; that is, pay no regard to the words feparately taken, but, conceiv-ing the idea, exprefs the whole in fuch terms as, in the language he is tranflating into, are appropriated to it.

Exact tranflation is rendered much more difficult by the accidental affociation of num-berlefs

berlefs foreign circumftances with the general meaning of words: For inftance, a
word being much ufed by people of low and
mean profeffions, may, from that circumftance only, be reputed mean and vulgar,
and be avoided by perfons of a liberal education ; and one word may be objected to,
as grofs and difgufting, and another be made
ufe of in preference to it, which conveys the
very fame idea, only in a lefs offenfive
manner.

This minute diftinction in the ufe of words
it is almoft impoffible to preferve in tranflating even from a modern and living language,
on account of the improbability there is, that
any words, in two languages, fhould have
both the fame general meaning, and the
fame accidental foreign affociations; but it
is abfolutely impoffible in tranflating from a
dead language, in which we have hardly any

U 3   means

means of tracing those accidental affociations.

This is a great advantage which the remains of a *dead language* have over writings
in a *living tongue.*   In the former it is impoffible to diftinguifh what is mean, vulgar,
and illiberal; every phrafe which is handed
down to us by ancient writers is received as
equally good and proper; in a courfe of time
thofe cafual affociations   are forgotten:
whereas time hath not done this kind of-
fice to the latter,   but many words and
phráfes, befides the principal idea they re-
préfent, convey to the minds of thofe who are
perfectly acquainted with every circumftance
in the ufe of them, a number of other ideas
which have no relation to the principal ones,
but which adhere infeparably to the words,
and may make the ufe of them very improper, when, otherwife, no objection could
have been made to them.

The

The humour of comedy and burlefque writing depends very much upon this minute diftinction in the ufe of words, as well as upon the changeable manners and cuftoms of particular places. In confequence of this circumftance, the moft delicate part of the wit of thefe writings is temporary, and local; and therefore impoffible to be preferved in a foreign and diftant tranflation.

Nothing fo directly tends to improve a language as the judicious tranflation of valuable polite writings of other languages into it. For it is eafy to fee that the language tranflated into, by this means, acquires the very fame power of expreffion with the language that is tranflated from.   Befides, the tranflator, having nothing but his ftyle to attend to, will probably make it more correct and harmonious than he could have done, if he

had

had had both the language and fentiment to attend to at the fame time.

Confidering tranflations in no other view than as ferving to improve the language into which they are made, they cannot be too free; that is, provided the whole fenfe of the author be communicated, and none of his ideas be loft or changed, it is an advantage that the fingle words, feparately taken, fhould not ftrictly correfpond to one another: for, by this means, each language retains its own characteriftick properties, while their power of expreffion is the fame.

LECTURE

LECTURE the SIXTEENTH.

OF

METRICAL

COMPOSITION.

THE firſt attempts towards ſpeech muſt have been automatic ſounds, excited by particular circumſtances, and little more than inarticulate expreſſions of fear, grief, joy, ſurprize, &c. *(a)* conſequently

---

(a) Notwithſtanding the powers of ſpeech might have been communicated, in a conſiderable degree, to the firſt parents of the human

quently men would at firſt ſpeak very loud
and ſtrong.   Agreeable to this, it is obſervable, that children, in their firſt attempts to
ſpeak, exert their whole ſtrength.   It is not
natural to ſpeak low, till ſpeaking have become not only perfectly voluntary, but e-
ven ſecondarily automatic, and aſſociated
with very ſlight preceding circumſtances.

From theſe principles it is natural to ſuppoſe that, while language was imperfect,
the buſineſs of ſpeech would be a matter of
more labour than it is at preſent; and that
mankind, in the firſt ages of the world,
would, from habit, continue for a conſiderable

race; yet, ſince it is natural to ſuppoſe it would
be only ſufficient for the purpoſes of their own
condition, we may perhaps conceive more juſtly
of the manner in which language was improved,
by ſuppoſing mankind to have begun from ſo
ſmall a beginning as is repreſented in the lecture.

able time that vehement articulation in which words were firſt learned.

The buſineſs of rude and ſimple ſpeech being a matter of ſo much labour to thoſe who firſt uſed a language, it cannot be ſuppoſed that *metre,* or *verſe* ſhould have been introduced till a conſiderable time after proſe had been in uſe. The latter is a matter of neceſſity, the former of ornament only. For *metrical compoſition* requires that words be placed in ſome regular order; ſo that the pronunciation of them may yield a kind of harmony. This, it is eaſy to ſee, requires ſome choice of words. Language, therefore, muſt not only have been formed, but have become pretty copious before it would admit of verſe.

The firſt verſes (like the rudiments of all other arts) were probably made by chance.

The

The harmony of words, at firſt caſually placed in metrical order, would engage the attention. The pleaſing ſenſation accompanying it would excite mankind, when they were firſt at leiſure to attend to their language, to conſider the nature and manner of it; from whence the tranſition to imitation is univerſally natural.

When verſe became tolerably familiar and eaſy, and before the art of writing was invented, it would ſoon be perceived to be an excellent vehicle to convey the knowledge of paſt tranſactions to poſterity; ſince verſes are eaſily committed to memory, and the regularity of the meaſure helps to prevent miſtakes in the repetition. Thus, in time, would moſt nations become ſtocked with traditional poems, ſerving for memorials of remarkable tranſactions; of which thoſe relating to their Gods and Heroes would

would be repeated and fung in their honour at their feſtivals. For the invention of *Muſick* and *Poetry* hath, in all nations, been nearly cotemporary; and there have always been methods of adapting the one to the other. The ſimple pronunciation of the ancients being flow and raiſed, muſt of itſelf have been muſical.

Things being in this ſituation, it is natural to ſuppoſe, that the firſt things men would think of committing to writing (after the art was invented by them, or communicated to them) would be theſe *poems;* and it might be ſome time before they would thinkof making uſe of the art for any other purpoſe. Accordingly, we find in hiſtory, that, in moſt nations, poems were the firſt compoſitions that were committed to writing, and that, the art of proſe-writing was ſubſe-

X   quent

quent to it. Sir *Isaac Newton* (I suppose upon the authority of *Strabo*) says that the *Greeks* wrote nothing in prose before the conquest of *Asia* by *Cyrus*, about which time *Pherecydes Scyrius*, and *Cadmus Milesius* introduced writing in prose.

Any one measure of verse being found out, it was easy to diversify it; and make it yield all the harmony it was capable of,

All the harmony that the *Ancients* ever attempted to give their language arose from the proper disposition of the syllables according to their *quantity*, as divided into *long* and *short*, two short syllables requiring the time of one long one. To exemplify this, take the following verses of *Virgil*.

Tityre, tu patulæ recubans sub tegmine fagi
Sylveſtrem tenui muſam meditaris avena.

All

All the harmony of thefe verfes confifts in the proper difpofition of the long and fhort fyllables. And, according to the more elaborate pronunciation of the ancients, the difference in the length of fyllables would be more obfervable than it is with us. This regard to quantity did not in the leaft interfere with the raifing or depreffing of the voice, which they called *Accent*.

On the contrary, according to our method of pronunciation, it is impoffible to diftinguifh the quantity and accent. We pronounce every fyllable with equal rapidity, except one fyllable in every word, which we pronounce with more force than the reft; which, doth, in fome meafure, of neceffity, occafion a production of the found. It is the regular fall of this accent that conftitutes the principal part of the harmony of all *European* verfes, as in the following in *Englifh*.

Say

Say why was man fo eminently raifed
Amid the vaft creation, why ordained
Through life and death to dart his piercing eye,
With thoughts beyond the limits of his frame?

Befides this, another kind of harmony
hath been introduced into moft modern languages; which is the fimilarity of found at
the clofe of the verfes, called *Rhyme*. The
following have this kind of harmony.

Know then this truth (enough for man to know)
Virtue alone is happinefs below.
The only point where human blifs ftands ftill,
And taftes the good without the fall to ill:
Where only merit conftant pay receives,
Is bleft in what it takes and what it gives.

Pope.

The principle therefore, or fource of
harmony, in ancient and modern poetry, is
totally different: the former arifes intirely
from quantity, the latter from the accent;
and fometimes accent in conjunction with
rhyme.

For

For this reason the ancient poetry was, of the two, the better adapted to musick; which is regulated chiefly by time, and perhaps the just pronunciation of verses, according to the natural length of the syllables (with a peculiar raised tone of voice, and such variations with regard to acute and grave as that manner of speaking would naturally throw the voice into) might be that in which the principal part of ancient vocal music consisted. Whereas, in modern music, (unless a long note be contrived to receive the accent through the whole verse, which is seldom done, except in some few songs) our poetry hath no more than an arbitrary connection with our music, and prose suits it quite as well: but to sing prose would have been reckoned very absurd among the *Ancients*, it being a thing that was never thought of or attempted by them.

X 3   Our

Our mufic, indeed, may be contrived to correfpond, in general, to the fentiment and paffion expreffed in a poem: for as the verfes may be of a diverting or mournful nature, the mufic may likewife, upon the whole, tend to infpire mirth or melancholy; but the particular words of the poem have ftill no real connection with the particular ftrains of the mufic. How often do we fee, in very good mufical compofitions, where words are fubjoined, the moft expreffive and important ftrains in the mufic to fall upon very trifling words in the poem. And do we not generally fing the fame notes to every ftanza of an ode; notwithftanding that the variation of the fentiment, and the different difpofition of the emphatical words in the line, feem to require a proportionable change in the notes that are fung with it: yet fo arbitrary and general is the connexion between our mufic and

and our poetry, that the abfurdity is not perceived.

Modern languages, and *Englijh* in particular, do not admit of the meafures of ancient poetry; becaufe the diftinction of our fyllables into long and fhort is not fufficiently apparent. According to the rules of ancient verfification, too great a number of them would be long. On the other hand, the leaft tendency to rhyme was condemned as vicious in ancient poetry; till, in fome late centuries, when the ancient pronunciation of the Latin was forgotten, fome *monks* compofed Latin verfes in rhyme, but without any regard to the quantity. One of them is faid to have turned the whole *Æneis of Virgil* into rhyme.

As the rules of verfification do necefarily confine a writer in the choice of his words,

poets,

poets, in all languages, take liberties which are not allowed to profe writers. This is called the *licentia poetica*, and makes the language of verfe differ confiderably from that of profe. In the *Italian* tongue this is very obfervable: for inftance, *anima*, in that language, fignifies *the foul*, in profe; when, in verfe, it is changed into *alma*.

LECTURE

LECTURE the SEVENTEENTH.

OBSERVATIONS.

ON THE

DIFFERENT PROPERTIES

OF

LANGUAGE.

TO avoid, as much as poſſible, all general and vague declamation in the compariſon of different languages, I ſhall, in the firſt place, lay down rules and criterions of the value of languages, and

ſubjoin

fubjoin examples to the obfervations I fhall make.

An attention to the ufe of language will inform us that, to the perfection of it, there muft concur the three following particulars. In the firft place it is neceffary there be a fufficient copia of words; fecondly that there be no ambiguities of words or conftructions; and, laftly, that the pronunciation of it be not grating, but pleafing to the ear. The two former of thefe criterions contribute to clear expreffion, and are therefore the fundamental properties of a good language; the latter is a matter of ornament only. Before I confider any language in particular, I fhall make fome general remarks upon each of the properties abovementioned, to prepare the mind to form a true judgment.

With

With refpect to the firft mentioned particular, a fufficient copia of words, it may be
obferved, that a language will neceffarily,
by fome means or other, increafe in proportion to the number of ideas and combinations of ideas to be expreffed by it; and that,
till, in confequence of the introduction of
arts and fciences, the ideas of a people be
increafed and diverfified, a copious language
would be fo far from being of ufe, that it
would be a great incumbrance to them.
Having no new ideas to exprefs by their
new words, numbers of them, if they were
ufed at all, muft become fynonymous. A
copious language therefore ought rather to
be confidered as an argument of the improvement of the nation that ufes it than
an encomium upon the language itfelf; the
latter being only a confequence of the
former.

Again

Again people equally cultivated upon the whole may excel in different refpects; of courfe the language of one nation will be more copious in fome things and more defective in others: fo that, upon the whole, the one may have no advantage over the other.

Moreover, it is poffible that a language may abound in words, the differences of which may be very fmall and infignificant; with refpect both to the found (being effected by a flight change of termination, &c.) and the ideas they convey. Such a language may abound in nimuteneffes, and yet not have the real compafs and extent of a language which hath fewer words but thofe more materially different. The chief advantage of the former language will be reaped by the *poet*, and the *orator;* as it will fupply them with a greater choice

choice of words without any materially fenfible difference in the ideas they convey.
The number of words in the *Englifh* language doth not exceed the number of words
in the *Greek;* and yet the arts and fciences
treated of in Englifh books demonftrate that,
having more knowledge, we have certainly
more ideas than they had. *(a)*

Secondly, a language fhould not be ambiguous. Upon this head it may be remarked that ambiguity may arife from two diftinct
caufes. In the firft place, the fame word
may be ufed to exprefs more ideas than one;
in which cafe the fenfe can only be deter-

Y   mined

***

(a) It is not however denied that minute
differences in the fignification of words are fometimes of confiderable ufe to *Philofophers;* who,
in refining upon vulgar fentiments and ideas,
have occafion to refine upon the vulgar language
too.

mined by its connection with other words;
as to *bear a child*, or to *bear a burden* or, as
is the practice in some nations, by different
tones and elevations of the voice, or different gestures of the body, accompanying the
pronunciation of the same word. Secondly,
ambiguity may arise from a want of sufficient methods to denote the several relations
of words to one another: for the sense of a
sentence depends as much upon the connection of the words, as the meaning of them
separately considered.

Sometimes the relations of words are expressed by other words appropriated to that
purpose; as (to) in the sentence, *He gave
the book* to *me*.   Sometimes the situation of
a word may serve to express its relation
to other words in the sentence, as *Alexander conquered Darius*, or the relation may
be

be expressed by the termination, as *Darium vicit Alexander.*

These are all the methods to prevent ambiguity, arising from a defective connection of words; upon which I would observe, that, in all these cases, provided the fundamental rules of a language be observed, ambiguity will be equally prevented: for, in whatever manner it be done, the relations will be actually denoted.

All the advantage of a language which hath recourse to the order and disposition of words to denote their relations, is, that it admits of no transpositions, for the purpose of the poet and orator, unless in sentences in which the sense itself will be sufficient to show the relation; as in this, *These things did Jesus*, or *Jesus did these things.* In whatever order these words be placed, though

Y 2   neither

neither termination nor particle expreſs the relation, no other than Jeſus can be imagined to be the agent; and the things referred to muſt have been done by him. In other caſes, when either term is naturally capable of being the agent or patient, ſuch a ſentence admits of no tranſpoſition.

It muſt, however, be remarked, that, when the difference of relation is expreſſed by the termination, the diſtinction by place is of no uſe; ſo that the means to prevent ambiguity is but ſingle in one caſe as well as in the other. For when the ſubject and attribute, for inſtance, have not been confined to one place more than another, the place cannot be conſidered as diſtinguiſhing them.

But the advantage of a language that expreſſes the relation of words by terminations,

above

above another that expresses the same relations with equal precision by particles prefixed, can only be in appearance, and the one
will admit of as much transposition as the
other. Because, as the particles accompany
the word, in the one case as strictly as the
terminations in the other, their relations to
other words will be known with equal certainty in any transposition: as *These things
did Jesus in Cana,* or *In Cana Jesus did
these things,* or *These things in Cana did
Jesus.* (a)

Y 3   If

(a) Had the modern *European* languages any
particle to distinguish the accusative from the
nominative they would with much greater precision admit equal degrees of transposition with the
Latin and *Greek,* as the less precision of the latter arises from hence, that different cases have
the same terminations. E. G. in Latin the *dative*
and *ablative* plural always, and sometimes singular are the same, in first declension the *nominative,*
vocative, and *ablative* are alike, in neuters, the

If it be faid, that fewer words are employed in one cafe than in the other, it is anfwered, that this makes no real difference, with refpect even to the pronunciation, and confequently the harmony, much lefs to perfpicuity: fince not only thofe particles, and the words they belong to, but all the words of an intire claufe of a fentence perfectly

---

nominative, vocative, and *accufative,* &c. This inconvenience is moreapparent in adjectives, thus *bona* is the *nominative, vocative,* and *ablative, feminine ;* and *nominative, vocative,* and *accufative plural* neuter: when therefore other words intervene between the fubftantive and its adjective the fenfe will hardly prefent itfelf at the firft reading, as in

Candida nec nigra cornua fronte geras.   *Ovid de trift.*   The Greek writers do likewife frequently place the prepofition after the cafe it governs, and fometimes at a confiderable diftancce from it. See an inftance Plut. Eth. p. 242.

In fome of thefe cafes, however, the difference of quantity would make a fufficient difference between words which were written with the fame letters, in the pronunciation of theancients.

fectly coalefce in pronunciation; there being, in fact, no greater interval between
word and word, than between fyllable and
fyllable: which was the reafon why languages were written anciently without any
diftinction of words. Suppofing, therefore,
that the fentences taken together confift of
the fame number of fyllables, and thofe
fyllables be capable of an equally eafy pronunciation, it makes no manner of difference, whether they be divided, mentally,
into words and particles, or into words with
terminations; fo that it cannot be the ufe
of articles, prepofitions, and auxiliary verbs,
in themfelves confidered, that makes
modern languages at all inferior to the
ancient.

Further, with refpect to precifion in the
ufe of words, it cannot be but that the words
of any language, after they have been ufed

a

a confiderable time, will acquire fome determinate meaning: and in how many different fenfes foever a word may happen to be
ufed, at the firft introduction of it, it is impoffible but that fome one acceptation, at
leaft in the fame conftruction, or fome few
analogous fenfes will prevail at laft, and all
other fignifications will grow into difufe. So
that it is in vain for any writer to pretend
that, in any language, which hath acquired a
fufficient copia of words, for the occafions
of thofe who ufe it, he cannot exprefs himfelf with accuracy and precifion, upon fuch
fubjects as the people who ufe it are accuf-
tomed to. No perfon can be at a lofs in this
refpect but for want of being acquainted
with the language he would ufe.

With refpect to modern *Eurepean* languages in general, and the *Englifh* and
French in particular; they have been fo
long

long ufed, without any confiderable alteration (which they would daily have received,
till they had arrived to a fufficient degree of
precifion, and fuch perfection as things of
this nature admit of) they abound with fo
many books upon all fubjects of human fpe-
culation, or human practice; that a perfon
who is mafter of all the powers of any of
them will be at no lofs to exprefs in it all
the conceptions and ideas he can wifh to
communicate, with the utmoft certainty of
being perfectly underftood by thofe who ufe
the fame language.

The laft mentioned criterion of a good
language is the eafe with which it is pronounced: for, certainly, a language is not
very eligible which requires a very violent
exertion of the organs of fpeech, or is incapable of poetical or oratorial harmony.
Upon this head I would obferve, that the
number

number of confonants compared with that of
the vowels, in the ordinary combinations of
them, in a language, is no certain criterion
of the harſhneſs or ſmoothneſs of it: for it
is very eaſy, by a proper poſition of them,
to make a word which hath a greater number of confonants in it be pronounced with
more eaſe, and found more agreeably than
one that hath fewer. How many confonants
are there to one vowel in the Engliſh word
ſtrand, and yet where is the harſhneſs of that
word? If we attend to the articulation, we
ſhall perceive, that the poſitions of the
tongue appropriated to thoſe confonants are
contiguous, and do not interfere with one
another: though it be certain that the poſition and motion of the organs of ſpeech may
be ſo complex, in pronouncing different
confonants together, as confiderably to impede the pronunciation; and therefore make
it more difficult to be pronounced though it

may

may not found very harsh when pronounced.
In this and the following cases let the impar-
tial ear be judge.

Secondly, a long syllable is not of itself
more disagreeable to the ear than a short one:
for instance, what is there more harsh in the
pronunciation of the words *stand*, or *blind*,
than *to* or *for*. Besides, a language that
hath not many complex *monosyllables* must
have more *polysyllabic words* to correspond
to them : for the simple monosyllabic combinations of letters are very few. So that
the difference of time in speaking different
languages is never worth regarding: for
instance *strength*, or *fortitude*. But the
rapid pronunciation, of every language,
particularly in common discourse, (which
naturally softens every harsh collision of the
consonants) renders almost all differences of
this kind wholly inconsiderable. This is
very

very remarkable in the *French* pronunciation which is not much more concife than
that of neighbouring languages, when fpoken full and deliberately.

Thirdly, imagination and deception have
much to do in the bufinefs of pronunciation;
fince we find that articulations which appear
harfh to one do not appear harfh to another.
For inftance, with how little reafon do
neighbouring nations complain of the difficulty of pronouncing the Englifh *th* as in
the words *that, then, thread.* The reafon
is that fuch a particular pofition of the organs of fpeech as the pronunciation of it
requires is unufual to them, and therefore
they muft take fome pains to learn it.

Perhaps none but a native can be a com-
petent judge of the harmony of his own language, and to him the articulations of it
can

can hardly ever appear harfh, whatever they
be abftractedly confidered: from being familiar, they are eafy.

The *Hebrew*, *Arabic*, and other *Eaftern* tongues are thought very fweet and me-
lodious in the countries where they are, or
have been, fpoken; and yet they abound
with *Gutterals*, and *Afpirates*, which, in
their own nature, are the moft difficult and
violent articulations that the human voice is
capable of. In the *Greek* frequent ufe
is made of   (anfwering to   in
Hebrew) alfo of   and   (none of which
were pronounced by the ancients as we now
pronounce them) and yet all people think
the *Greek* to have been a very harmonious
mufical language.

Fourthly, we muft not judge concerning
the harmony of a language from the ufe

that is actually made of it by any one writer, but a number of the beft, who had the
moft command of it: for we fee, in our
own tongue, that the difference between two
writers, in point of harmony of ftyle, is
often almoft as great as between two different
languages.

Fifthly, The real ftructure of a compleatly harmonious language muft be fuch
as will admit of any words or number of
words to fucceed one another with eafe, as
if they were one word.   Too many confonants therefore muft not be thrown either
to the beginnings or the endings of words:
otherwife, though the words, fingly taken,
may not found difagreeably; yet, when
combined with others like themfelves, the
concourfe of fuch a prodigious number of
confonants at the end of one word and the
beginning of the next may not only impede
the

the pronunciation, and interrupt the found, but embarras the organs of fpeech, and make the articulation harfh and difagreeable.

Having premifed thefe general obfervations and criterions, we may with the greater eafe, clearnefs, and certainty, characterize the feveral languages that gentlemen of a liberal education have occafion to make themfelves acquainted with, or make ufe of.

LECTURE

LECTURE the EIGHTEENTH.

A

COMPARISON

OF

DIFFERENT LANGUAGES.

THE *Hebrews* were a people who, till their language was fixed, were, in a manner, ftrangers to the arts and fciences; they lived generally under an abfolute monarchy, and, in their whole hiftory there occurs not one period in which eloquence, or the art of fpeaking in public, is taken notice

notice of. Though, therefore, we know not the whole extent of their language; nothing but the *facred books* being come down to us, we may naturally conjecture, it could not have been a very copious one.

With refpect to its ftructure, it is remarkably fimple and regular, confidering the number of its inflexions. It is, however, in fome things fuperfluous, and in others defective; but thefe apprehended fuperfluities and defects are not peculiar to it, but common to it and moft other Eaftern languages; and, being fo general in that part of the world, it is poffible that they may be no inconvenience, but rather peculiarly fuited to the manners and occafions of the people that ufe them.

The moft remarkable fuperfluity is the *genders of verbs*, and of the *perfonal pro-*
Z 3   *nouns;*

nouns; and its moſt remarkable defect
ſeems to be, that it is in a manner wholly
incapable of *compounding* its words; though
it excells all others in the exactneſs and regularity of the ſimple derivation of the
greater part of its words from a few roots.
It ſeems alſo very extraordinary that a language which deſcends even to genders in its
inflexion of verbs ſhould have no caſes for
nouns, and that its preter and future tenſes
ſhould be uſed promiſcuouſly by the uſe of
the *converſivum.*

The *Hebrew* having no caſes for nouns,
admits of few tranſpoſitions: and, on that
account, cannot be well adapted to the purpoſes of verſe: yet, on the other hand,
ſince both nouns and verbs admit of a great
variety of prefixes and ſuffixes, the words
ſeem calculated to intermix with one another without any diſagreeable hiatus, or ſenſible embaraſſment in the pronunciation; a
thing

thing greatly favourable to verfification. It may likewife be fubjoined in this place, that the poetical parts of the *Old Teſtament* excell the poetry of all other nations in fublime conceptions and ſtriking metaphors, which are the life and foul of true poetry. The *meaſure of verſe* in this language is wholly unknown.

This language hath a fingular advantage in the ſtructure of its verbs, fince by means of its *Pihil, Hiphil,* and *Hithpahel* feveral very important modes of an affirmation may be expreſſed with wonderful concifenefs and energy.

Hebrew is probably one of the moſt ancient languages in the world: for we can difcover no traces of its derivation from any other language whatever. Similar it is to other Eaſtern tongues, but which of them

was

was the *mother-tongue*, it is impoſſible, for want of ſufficient data in ancient hiſtory, to determine. It is in every reſpect a dead language, being neither ſpoken by any people on earth, nor read but for the ſake of underſtanding the books of the Old Teſtament, which are written in it.

GREECE was the mother of ſcience and of arts to this weſtern part of the world: conſequently, the language of Greece is the fountain from which all our terms in thoſe arts and ſciences which were known in Greece are derived. It continued to be ſpoken for the ſpace of many centuries, each of which abounded with *Orators*, *Poets*, *Hiſtorians*, and *Philoſophers;* whoſe conſtant ſtudy it was to uſe it to the moſt advantage. It was alſo ſpoken a great part of this time by many independant and rival ſtates.

The

The natural confequence of thefe circumftances was a redundancy of words, and
conftructions, and prodigious dialectick differences in the pronunciation and ufe of
words.

It feems furprizing that, notwithftanding
this manifeft redundancy of Greek words,
many hundreds of them are no otherwife to
be diftinguifhed from one another but by
their accent (the characters of which were
unknown to the ancients) as   , *vita;*
and   , *arcus.* And in one intire fet
of compound words, the accent alone determines whether they are to be underftood in
an active or a paffive fenfe.   Thus
is *matricida,* one who kills his mother, and
                is *a matre occifus,* one who
is killed by his mother.

There is, likewife, a great redundancy
of

of Greek *tenfes:* at leaft it is impoffible for us to conceive how time paft, for the ufe of fpeech, could be divided into eight diftinct parts: for fo many preterite tenfes of an active fignification (including thofe of the middle voice) the Greek verbs have. And indeed, to judge from the actual practice of Greek writers, we cannot perceive but they ufed many of them promifcuoufly.

There is too great a latitude in the fyntax of the language: fo that it requires fome time before a perfon can get acquainted with the particular manner of conftruction ufed by a new author, fo as toread him with eafe or almoft with underftanding. And in the moft celebrated and valuable authors, fo much is crowded into a fentence, the claufes are fo diflocated, and the conftruction fo perplexed (a mark of exceffive refinement in writing, as was obferved before of

the

the concatenation of fentenees) that few who learn Greek are ever able to mafter them thoroughly. This is the cafe particularly with *Thucydides,* and *Demofthenes.*

In confequence of the prodigious variety of words in this language, and the remarkable eafe with which they run into all poffible combinations, it admits of the utmoft precifion, and the moft minute diftinctions in our conceptions may be expreffed in it. This however renders tranflation from Greek peculiarly difficult, for want of terms in other languages to exprefs fo many degrees and fhades, as it were, of ideas.

On account of the happy mixture of vowels and confonants, the unequalled copia of words, their eafy concurrence, and unparallelled tranfpofition, in *Greek,* no poet, orator, or writer in general, could have a
language

language more to his wish, when once he was perfectly master of it: but the extent and intricacy of it (notwithstanding there be many pretenders to the knowledge of it) will keep the riches and powers of it unknown, except to a few in modern times.

Greek is a dead language, and hardly any attempt to write in it at this day; and indeed one language is surely sufficient for the correspondence of the learned: but there are a prodigious number of books extant in it, of unspeakable value for the cultivation of the human mind, and containing the greatest masterpieces of *Poetry, Oratory, History,* and moral *Philosophy.*

The language seems to be original, both with respect to its words and construction, as we are not acquainted with any older language similar to it. The words that it

said

said to have borrowed from the Eastern tongues are very few.

The Greeks were taught the use of let-ters by *Cadmus*, who is said to have been a *Phenician*. But as he left *Asia* about the time of *David*'s conquest of *Idumea* (which was probably the nation that first of all dis-tinguished itself for its application to the arts and sciences) and many of the inhabitants, being obliged to abandon their country, took shipping at *Tyre* and *Sidon* in order to seek their fortunes in the west, it is not im-probable that he might have been an *Edomite*.

The LATIN tongue doth, in many re-spects, bear evident marks of a Greek ori-ginal, the Latin *declensions*, *inflections* of *verbs*, and *syntax*, which are the stamina of a language, are analogous to the Greek as far as they go. The Roman letters, and

A a

a great number of their oldeſt words, ſuch as pronouns, &c. (which, from the nature of the thing, muſt have been coeval with the firſt riſe of the language) are likewiſe Greek. The founders of *Rome*, having been ſeparated from the Greeks before the letters invented by *Simonides* were generally received, the Latin alphabet varies in ſome reſpects from the Greek. The Roman colonies were alſo planted before the ſtructure of the Greek language was ſo complex as it afterwards grew to be, became intermixed and incorporated with ſeveral nations of *Italy*, and roaming *Celtes*, and continued many hundred years in a ſtate next to perfect barbarity, without paying the leaſt attention to their language. On theſe accounts, the internal ſtructure of the language is much leſs complex than the Greek, and leans more to the ſimplicity of the northern tongues.

The

The Latin tongue continued very rough and barren till the introduction of the Grecian arts and sciences into Rome, from their acquaintance with which the Romans derived all the copia and harmony of their own language. All *technical* Latin terms relating to the sciences and the more elegant arts are intirely *Greek*, and many *Greek* words, which the *Roman* writers had occasion to make use of, (that either could not well be expressed by *Roman* letters, or which, by reason of their termination, or on any other account, did not incorporate very easily with their own tongue) it was customary for them to intermix, pure Greek as they were, in their own Latin compositions; and probably in their discourses too. This practice began about *Cicero*'s time, in whose works many specimens of it may be seen, and especially in his epistles.

The

The *Latin* falls greatly fhort of the *Greek* with refpeḋ to the facility of the compofition of words, notwithftanding it retains a confiderable power of diverfifying their fignification by the ufe of prepofitions, &c. and it hath a fufficient number of *diminutives*. From the *Northern Languages*, it derives a greater proportion of confonants than the *Greek;* but is ftill fufficiently harmonious for the purpofe of verfification.

The *Romans*, having one feat of power and of arts, allowed of no dialeḋs; which makes their language the more uniform and regular, and the more eafy to be learned. It hath very little of that ambiguity and intricacy in its ftruḋure that is complained of in the Greek, and being nearer to the medium between the extremes of fimplicity and refinement, feems of the two to be much

better

better adapted to the general ufe of mankind.

Had the Romans continued a longer time
unmixed with barbarous nations, and arts
and fciences flourifhed fome centuries longer
at Rome, the Latin tongue could not have
failed to acquire a copia of words equal, in
ufe and value, if not in number, to that of
the Greek; at the fame time that it would
have improved itfelf in point of regularity,
and analogy with it felf; which the ftate of
Greece would never have admitted in their
language: on the contrary, the Greek language neceffarily grew continually more various and unlike itfelf. But, through an un-
fortunate turn of events, it happened that the
Roman language was fpoken in its purity little longer than one intire century; after which
it became greatly corrupted, and was ab-

folutely a dead language, long before the
Greek.

Upon the revival of learning in the weft,
the *Latin* became the only language of the
Literati in *Europe*, who hardly made ufe
of any other either in converfation or in
writing.   Since the cultivation of the modern
tongues, it hath not been fo much ufed; but
ftill it is highly difreputable, in a perfon of
a fcholaftic profeffion, not to be able to exprefs himfelf correctly in it upon occafion.

The *Roman claffics* are not perhaps, upon the whole, inferior to the *Greek*; but
the really valuable Latin authors are much
fewer than the Greek: and, without underftanding Greek, it is in vain to pretend to a
thorough knowledge of Latin.   The ruins
of the Latin tongue have greatly enriched all
the

the modern European languages, and do ſtill contribute to their improvement.

The modern *French*, *Italian*, and *Spaniſh* tongues have fewer inflections of words than the *Latin;* but more than the *German*, and *Engliſh*. For though, originally, the ſame *Celtick* language was ſpoken in all thoſe countries; yet, in conſequence of the greater proximity of *Spain* and *Gaul* to Rome, and the more intimate and longer intercourſe of the nations, the languages of thoſe countries have deviated conſiderably from their original principles; whereas the *Engliſh* has only borrowed *Latin* words to incorporate with its own, and the *German* hath, even in that reſpect, borrowed little from the *Latin*.

The *German* language ſeems to be but little removed from its ancient barbarity.

The

The *French* and *Italian* have attained to their *ne plus ultra;* and the *Englifh* feems to be as near to its meridian as poffible.

The *French* fyntax hath been made more intricate than formerly by a greater multiplicity of rules than ufe required, and the peculiarity of its accent and pronunciation hath an unfavourable effect upon its poetry; as it makes it incapable of that variety which is neceffary to true harmony, at the fame time that, in common with all other European languages, it makes no ufe of the quantity of fyllables in verfe.

The fplendour of the *French monarchy*, at a time when language had begun to be attended to in Europe, and it became in a manner neceffary to ufe fome one language in the forms of public tranfactions, contributed to recommend the *French* as the *political*

tical language of *Europe* : it likewife introduced it into the *European courts* ; and it is
alfo now become in a great meafure the
common language of *merchants*.

The *Italian,* of all the modern tongues,
is the beft adapted to mufic : for the ftructure of the language is fuch as gives the
freeft play to the vowels, there feldom oc-
curring fuch a concourfe of confonants in it
as can ftraiten or confine the paffage of the
found.

It doth not feem poffible that any of the
modern languages (according to the ftate of
improvement in the arts and fciences) fhould
want words. Whenever the want of new
terms was perceived by a people, had they
nothing to have recourfe to but the common
ftock that nature hath lodged in the variety
of articulation that the human voice is capable

ble of, they would foon fupply themfelves: how much more eafy then is it to introduce words already appropriated to the very ideas they want to exprefs, either from the dead languages, or fome of the living neighbouring ones. Accordingly we find that we are ftill borrowing words occafionally from other tongues, and the neceffity or convenience of this practice will foon eftablifh fuch words, notwithftanding all the clamour that may be made againft innovations.

LECTURE

LECTURE the NINETEENTH.

OF THE

ORIGIN, USE,

AND

CESSATION

OF

DIVERSITY

OF

LANGUAGES.

THE race of mankind having, according to the Old Testament history, had one origin, must have spoken one language, and this would continue to be spoken

ken

ken without much variation while their numbers would permit them to refide near together.

The prefent diverfity of languages is generally believed to have taken its rife from the building of *Babel*, and to have been brought about by the interpofition of the divine being: But it is no impiety to fuppofe, that this (agreeable to moft other operations of the deity) might have been brought about by natural means. The poffibility of this natural deviation feems to be deduced from the following confiderations.

Firft, The primitive language, or that which was fpoken by the firft family of the human race, muft have been very fcanty, and infufficient for the purpofes of their defcendants, in their growing acquaintance with the world.

Secondly,

Secondly, Not being fixed by the prac-tice of writing, it would be very liable to variation.

Thirdly, Suppofing the primitive lan-guage to have had few inflections (becaufe few would have been fufficient) it would eafily admit any inflections which chance or defign might fuggeft to the firft founders of different families, or to their fucceffors. Thefe different inflections would confe-quently introduce different conftructions of words, and different rules of fyntax: and thus what are called the very *ftamina* of languages would be formed independantly of one another, and admit of all poffible varieties.

Fourthly, Confidering into what different climates mankind were difperfed, furnifhed with the bare rudiments of the art of fpeech,

Bb   into

into what different ways of living they fell, and how long they continued without the art of writing (without which no language can be fixed) it feems to be no wonder that languages fhould be fo different as they are; both with refpect to the rules of inflection, with the fundamentals of Grammar which depend upon them, and the words of which they confift.

The difficulty which fome alledge there is in conceiving how languages fhould arife in the world fo very different, not only in the words, but in the manner of ufing them, feems to arife wholly from the fuppofition, that the primitive language was copious, regular, and perfect in all its parts: the difficulty of changing fuch a language is allowed; but the fact, it is apprehended, is much eafier accounted for upon the prefent hypothefis.

To

To thefe arguments it may be added that, to a perfon thoroughly acquainted with the prefent ftate of mankind, the prodigious diverfity of human manners and cuftoms may probably appear almoft as difficult to be accounted for as the diverfity of languages only.

Different languages being formed, in this manner, long ufe, and much more writing, would, at length, fix them; but leave them ftill fubject to the changes and revolutions that have been mentioned, and accounted for, in a preceding lecture.

This diverfity of languages is generally complained of as a great inconvenience to the human race, in that it prevents fo free a communication as there otherwife would be among men. This may be allowed, and yet, upon the whole, this diverfity of lan-

Bb 2   guages

guages may have been of great advantage to us; both as individuals and a collective body.

In the first place, diversity of languages and diversity of government (the one in a great measure contributing to the other) tended to check the propagation of vice and false religion in the early ages of the world. This would help to prevent the establishment of any one species of idolatry in the world, which might have taken place in consequence of one common language, and one empire, or much larger empires, and of longer duration than any that have actually subsisted. Whereas, divided as the state of the world hath been, no superior degree of credit was given to any species of false religion more than to another; by which means, their mutual absurdities have been more easily exposed, and true religion hath had a fairer opportunity of establishing itself.
Secondly,

Secondly, The Study of different languages hath a moſt happy influence upon the human mind, in freeing it from many prejudices and errors, which ariſe from verbal aſſociations and analogies. We ſee that perſons who have no knowledge of more than one language are perpetually confounding the ideas of words with the ideas of things; which the compariſon of languages, and frequent rendering from one into another, helps to make us diſtinguiſh.

We ſee, in particular, with what difficulty and uncertainty perſons who have learned only their native tongue diſtinguiſh the parts of ſpeech, for want of attending to the different kinds of ideas which they repreſent. Let the experiment be tried upon a perſon of good underſtanding, and it will found a conſiderable time, and in conſequence of very cloſe thinking, that he

Bb 3   can

can learn to diftinguifh the moft obvioufly
diftinct parts, as *fubftantives*, *adjectives*,
and *verbs :* and perhaps he will diftinguifh
them, at laft, rather by their circumftances,
and adjuncts, than by an attention to the
nature of the ideas they prefent to his mind.
For inftance, he will diftinguifh an *adjective*, by its admitting *man* or *thing* after it *;*
a *fubftantive* by its taking *good* or *bad* before it, and a *verb* by its being preceded by
the perfonal pronouns *I*, *thou*, *he*, &c. and
not by confidering that a *fubftantive* is a
name of a thing; an *adjective*, a property;
and a *verb*, an affirmation. And, as in
this, fo, for the fame reafon, it is eafy to
fee that, in every other refpect, the comparifon of different languages muft be of infinite fervice to us in helping us to difen-
tangle and diftinguifh our ideas.

How many of the abfurdities of the *Greek
philofo-*

philosophers, of all sects, are we now able to trace up to verbal analogies? the *Latin* tongue was too ne r the *Greek* to be of much service to the Romans in this respect. How many of those controversies in christianity, which arose before the propagation of learning in the west, are, at the bottom, merely verbal? How many of them were exploded upon the first revival of learning and the study of languages? and how many are still exploded by the same means at this day? These facts demonstrate the unspeakable advantage of the study of different languages. To appearance, this is an affair of *words* only; but these words are, more closely than men imagine, connected with *things*, and things of considerable consequence.

To this, let me add that, it were almost impossible that the nature and rationale of language should have been understood, while

it

it had continued one and invariable. The little light that hath yet been ftruck out upon the fubject of language in general hath refulted from the comparifon of the properties of different languages actually fubfifting. For want of the grounds of this univerfal language being thoroughly underftood, it could hardly have been ufed with precifion in many particular cafes; let it, originally, have been ever fo perfect; and mankind, having no general principles of language to have recourfe to, to help them to correct and adjuft it, as new occurrences arofe; it is not impoffible but that the inconveniences of this one univerfal language might ultimately, have exceeded thofe arifing from the ufe of different languages.

It may, likewife, give fome additional evidence to a fpeculative mind in favour of thefe arguments, to confider how analogous
thofe

thofe fuppofed benefits arifing from the diverfity of languages are to the reft of the works of nature: fince we have reafon believe that all *evils*, whether neceffary to, or permitted in this world, are both *temporary*, and, while they continue, *falutary*; that is, relatively fo, and the ftate of every thing connected with them confidered.

There have been fome men of learning who flattered themfelves with the profpect of the intire ceffation of this diverfity of languages; and feveral projects have been fet on foot to conftruct one *philofophical language*, which fhould be adaquate to all the purpofes of fpeech, and be without thofe fuperfluities, defects, and ambiguities, either in words or ftructure, with which all languages actually abound. This language, it is fuppofed, would recommend itfelf to the *literati* for the eafe and precifion attending

the

the ufe of it, and by degrees become the language of the whole world.

The moft rational plan of an univerfal and philofophical language is that which Dr. *Wallis* hath delineated in his elaborate treatife upon the fubject, and of which the following is a fketch.

Having in the firft place, with prodigious labour and exactnefs, diftributed all things to which names are given into claffes, under forty genufes or general heads (fome of which however are fubordinate to others) he affigns a fhort and fimple character to each of thefe forty genufes, a definite variation of the character to each difference under the genufes, and a further variation for each fpecies, &c. By this means the characters reprefenting all things that have names have

the

the fame analogies with one another that the things themfelves have.

Characters being provided for the names of things, the Grammatical diftinctions of words, *numbers tenfes, perfons, voices,* &c. are denoted by fome appendage to the character.

In this manner may we be furnished with an univerfal character, which fhall reprefent ideas directly without the intervention of any founds, and which may be equally underftood by people ufing any language whatever.

To make this character effable, the Doctor appropriates a fingle found to the characters reprefenting each genus and difference, and alfo to each variation and appendage before mentioned : and they are

fo

fo contrived, that the fimple founds adapted to all the parts of the moft complex
character may be pronounced with eafe as
one word.

By this means any people, after they
had applied this character to reprefent their
ideas, might foon learn to read it in the
fame manner as any other people; whereby, in converfation as well as in writing,
they might make themfelves perfectly underftood by one another.

The elements of this character and
language are fo few, and the combination
of them fo eafy, that the doctor fays he
doth not doubt, but that "a perfon of a
"good capacity and memory may, in one
"months fpace, attain to a good readinefs
"of expreffing his mind this way, either in
"the character or language."

As

As the names of individuals cannot be comprehended in tables of genufes and their differences, the doctor hath contrived an *alphabet* of all the fimple articulations of the human voice; to which he hath affigned two fets of characters, to be ufed at pleafure : the one confifts of fhort and plain ftrokes, the other is a kind of delineation of the pofition of the organs in forming the articulations.

Whenever this noble project is refumed, it feems to be impoffible to proceed upon a better plan than this. The principal thing that is wanting to the perfection of it is a more perfect diftribution of things into claffes than, perhaps, the prefent ftate of knowledge can enable us to make.

At prefent likewife, language itfelf, as an abftract fcience, is not fufficiently underftood to fucceed in fo grand a fcheme; and

Cc whether

whether the prefent diverfity of languages will, in any finite time, have anfwered all the ends it is capable of, and the ceffation of it be defirable, is what we have not as yet *data* fufficient to determine with certainty.   Otherwife, that fuch a defign may be effeɛted, in fome diftant ages of the world, when the powers of language and of nature fhall be more perfeɛtly underftood, doth not feem fo improbable as many of the prefent aɛtual difcoveries in *philofophy* muſt have feemed to all men, but a century ago.

Perhaps the analogy of nature may give us fome encouragement to expeɛt fuch an event.   For fince all other evils and inconveniences have *final caufes*, which terminate by the means of thofe very evils, the diverfity of languages, when it hath compleatly anfwered all the prefent ufes of it, may alfo contribute to its own extermination.

REFEREN-

REFERENCES.

THE books to which I would refer the ftudent, who is defirous of mak-ing himfelf more perfectly acquainted with feveral of the fubjects treated of in this courfe, are thofe mentioned below.

The famenefs of method, unavoidable in fuch a fubject, makes references to particu-lar parts of the *general treatifes* quite fuper-fluous; and the fubjects of the other treatifes are mentioned in the lift itfelf.

From *Reland* I was fupplied with a great part of thofe notes which relate to the peculiarities in the ftructure of fome of the *Indian* and *American* languages. If the author

author had had the good fortune to meet with more books (which are probably extant) of the fame kind; viz. which treat of the peculiarities of foreign tongues, he would have had an opportunity of making this treatife much more valuable and entertaining. If any perfon, into whofe hands this performance may accidentally fall, would direct him to fuch books, he will thankfully acknowledge the favour.

A general and rational grammar, by Meffieurs de port royal; as alfo their Latin, and Greek grammars.

Harris's Hermes.

Bayley's introduction to Languages.
Robertfon's method of reading Hebrew.
[Introduction.

Hartley on man. Ch. 3d. Section I. of
words

words, and the ideas affociated with them.

Du Frefne's Gloffary of the modern Greek. Preface.

Hadrian Reland's mifcellaneous differtations, vol. 3d.

Richards's Welch Grammar, & Dictionary.

Wilkins's Effay towards a real Character and philofophical language.

Brerewood on Languages.

Sharpe's two differtations on the origin, conftruction, divifion, and relation of languages; and the original powers of letters.

Had the author feen this laft ingenious performance in time, he would not have afferted as at p. 276, that the words which the Greeks are faid to have borrowed from the eaftern languages were very few.

A GEN-

A General Table of

CONTENTS.

LECT.

CONTENTS. 307

LEC-

CONTENTS.

LEC-

LECTURE XIV.

LECTURE XV.

                                            The

   Of

E R R A T A.

Page	Line	for	read
20	11	feem	feems.
24	10	is	are.
35	10	fhould have the ideas	fhall have the idea
50	21	men	man.
65	6	than	than words.
68	12	*Danube*	the *Danube*.
69	5	*Plural*	the *Plural*.
71	2 Note.	*clamat*	*ædificavit*
88	3 Note.	hath	have.
95	12 Note.	other	others.
106	11	*ame, ames*	*aime, aimes*.
109	22 Note.	*into*	*in to*.
116	19	are	is.
121	14	praiphrafes	periphrafes.
131	9	*mutair*	*mutari*.
136	10	*Boetians*	*Bœotians*.
140	8	reprefent	reprefents.
154	3, 10, &c.	concatention	concatenation.
156	9	augmentative	argumentative.
157	2	late	later.
ib.	8	*Thucidides*	*Thucydides*.
ib.	9	*Zenophon*	*Xenophon*.
159	13, 14	*was*	*were*.
160	17	*Delphin*	*Delphic*.
163	2	many	may
167	7	*ars*	*pars*.
170	17	kind	kinds.
174	9	*Roftra*	*Roftrata*.
184	17	whereever	whatever.
199	4	for	form.
204	12	though	(though. [that.
209	6	obfervable that even	even obfervable
249	6	LANGUAGE	LANGUAGES.
263	16	*fortitude*	*fortitudo*.
273	10	but	than.
277	10	and	when.
297	4	believe	to believe.